God's Promises FULFILLED:
THE END TIMES PROPHECY

God's Promises FULFILLED:
THE END TIMES PROPHECY

Paul J. Headington

Kingdom Publishers

God's Promises Fulfilled: The End Times Prophecy

Copyright© Paul J. Headington

All rights reserved. No part of this book may be
reproduced in any form by photocopying or any
electronic or mechanical means, including information
storage or retrieval systems, without permission in
writing from both the copyright owner and the publisher of the book.
The right of Paul j. Headington to be identified as the author
of this work has been asserted by him in
accordance with the Copyright, Designs and Patents Act
1988 and any subsequent amendments thereto.
A catalogue record for this book is available from the
British Library.

All Scripture Quotations have been taken from the New Kings James version of the Bible

ISBN: 978-1-911697-70-1

1st Edition by Kingdom Publishers, London, UK.

You can purchase copies of this book from any leading bookstore or email
contact@kingdompublishers.co.uk

I dedicate my book to my loving wife Hayley, my beautiful daughter, & in loving memory to my parents John and June.

Holy Bible (New Kings James Version)

John 3:16

16 "For God so loved the world that He gave His only begotten Son, that whoever believes in Him should not perish but have everlasting life."

Malachi, Chapter 3:6

6 "For I am the Lord, I do not change"

Table of Contents

Forward	1
1. Introduction	5
a. What Is Man?	8
b. Why Are We Here?	8
c. Where Are We Going?	9
d. I Must Choose	9
2. God	11
a. God	13
b. Authority in Christianity	16
c. God's Creation	20
3. The Downfall of Lucifer/The Angel of Light	25
4. The Old Testament	33
a. The Old Testament	35
b. The books of the Law, History, Poetry and Prophecy	36
c. The Fall of Mankind and Why?	39
d. Sin, what changed?	40
e. God's Commandments, Judgements and Laws	43
f. The Ten Commandments	47
g. Bible verses about Judgement	49

h. Abomination to God's laws	56
5. The New Testament	**75**
a. The New Testament	77
b. The Two Covenants	80
c. Jesus Christ, The Son of God, The Saviour	84
d. Faith	88
e. Repentance	91
f. Confession	94
g. Baptism	97
h. The Church, Part 1	100
i. The Church, Part 2	104
j. The Genealogy from Adam to Jesus Christ	109
6. Final: The End Times Prophecy	**117**
a. The Second Coming of Christ	120
b. Daniel and King Nebuchadnezzar's Dream	123
c. The Medo-Persian Empire	130
d. Daniel and Revelation: The Four Beasts	132
e. Hell	149
f. Heaven	151
7. References	**153**

Forward

Welcome and thank you, for choosing to read this book.

The rationale I have adopted when writing this book, is that it must be one hundred percent based upon biblical fact, God's Holy Word, The Bible (New Kings James Version).

The Bible shows the intent and baseline to how we should all live our lives, in accordance with God's merciful and graceful love, through His Commandments, Judgements and Laws, that through believing on God's Son, Jesus Christ our sins will be forgiven.

As NKJV, **John 3:16-18** *clearly states:*
> *16 For God so loved the world that He gave His only begotten Son, that whoever believes in Him should not perish but have everlasting life. 17 For God did not send His Son into the world to condemn the world, but that the world through Him might be saved.*
>
> *18 "He who believes in Him is not condemned; but he who does not believe is condemned already, because he has not believed in the name of the only begotten Son of God.*

The Bible is God's prophetic word, where God has provided mankind with a clear set of instructions of how we should live, within the boundaries of knowing what is right and what is outside God's natural law i.e. sin.

God chose prophets and teachers to deliver His message, so that we share eternal life with Him after our mortal lives have ended on this earth. God wants everyone to live for eternity with Him upon the New Heaven and New Earth.

NKJV, Revelation 21:1-7
All Things Made New

21 Now I saw a new heaven and a new earth, for the first heaven and the first earth had passed away. Also there was no more sea. 2 Then I, John, saw the holy city, New Jerusalem, coming down out of heaven from God, prepared as a bride adorned for her husband. 3 And I heard a loud voice from heaven saying, "Behold, the tabernacle of God is with men, and He will dwell with them, and they shall be His people. God Himself will be with them and be their God. 4 And God will wipe away every tear from their eyes; there shall be no more death, nor sorrow, nor crying. There shall be no more pain, for the former things have passed away."

5 Then He who sat on the throne said, "Behold, I make all things new." And He said to me, "Write, for these words are true and faithful."

6 And He said to me, "It is done! I am the Alpha and the Omega, the Beginning and the End. I will give of the fountain of the water of life freely to him who thirsts. 7 He who overcomes shall inherit all things, and I will be his God and he shall be My son."

This book concentrates on end time prophetic statements and events, those which have already occurred, with particular emphasis on end times prophecy, as mentioned in the books of Daniel and Revelation, for the last empire has yet to reveal itself, only when the Holy Spirit's veil is removed:

2 Thessalonians 2:7-12
> *"For the mystery of lawlessness is already at work; only He who now restrains will do so until He is taken out of the way.* ***8*** *And then the lawless one will be revealed, whom the Lord will consume with the breath of His mouth and destroy with the brightness of His coming.* ***9*** *The coming of the lawless one is according to the working of Satan, with all power, signs, and lying wonders,* ***10*** *and with all unrighteous deception among those who perish, because they did not receive the love of the truth, that they might be saved.* ***11*** *And for this reason God will send them strong delusion, that they should believe the lie,* ***12*** *that they all may be condemned who did not believe the truth but had pleasure in unrighteousness."*

Therefore, I ask the reader, to examine the contents of this book with their Holy Bibles when reading.

I have referred every biblical book name from the Old and New Testaments, with chapter(s) or verse's (or both); using the New Kings James Version as the chosen version of the Holy Bible.

(Additionally, to supplement your reading, there is also a detailed biblical timeline provided. The timeline provides historical evidence of past, present, and future events illustrated in the Bible.)

God bless, and always remember God loves you!

BIBLICAL TIMELINE

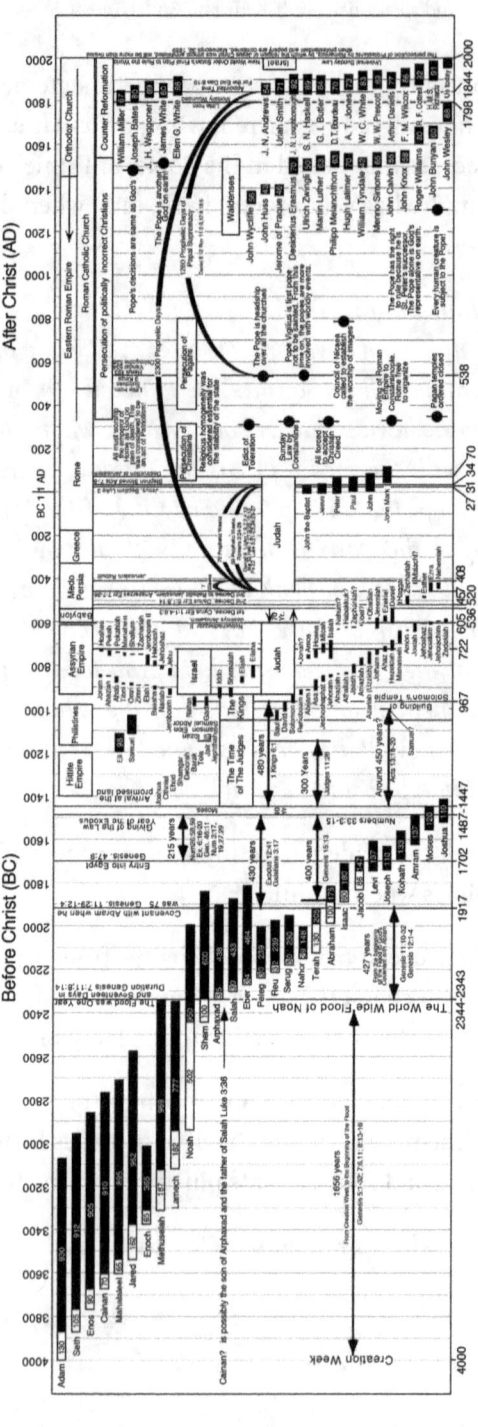

CHAPTER 1

Introduction

1. Introduction

Long ago, King David asked God: *"What is man that you are mindful of him, and the son of man that You visit him?"* (*Psalms 8:4*). People have many things in common with animals. They breathe the same air. They eat similar food. They have many of the same needs. But people are different from animals.

Because people are different from animals, we want to know why we are here. What is our purpose on this earth? Since we know that we only live a few short years, how should we use our time? Should we live only to satisfy the needs of our bodies? Should we spend our time looking for the pleasure of this world?

Because we are different from animals, we want to know where we are going when we die. Life on earth is very short. Job said: *"Man who is born of woman is of few days and full of trouble. He comes forth like a flower and fades away; he flees like a shadow and does not continue"* (*Job 14:1-2*). Are we the same as animals when we die? Do we just breathe our last breath and then there is nothing?

How can we find the answer to these questions? The only One who can give us the answers is God, Who created us. The answers are found in His book, the Bible. In the Bible, God has told us who we are, why we are here on earth, and where we will go when we die.

a. What Is Man?

What is man? What makes people different from animals? The Apostle Paul answered this question when he wrote to the Christians in Thessalonica: *"Now may the God of peace Himself sanctify you completely; and may your whole spirit, soul, and body be preserved blameless at the coming of our Lord Jesus Christ"* (*1 Thessalonians 5:23*). Animals have physical bodies only. But every person has a spirit within his body. Our bodies will die, decay, and return to the dust from which the first man, Adam, was made (***Genesis 3:19; Genesis 35:18; James 2:26***). But the spiritual part of man will continue to live. The Bible says: *"Then the dust* (our bodies) *will return to the earth as it was, and the spirit* (the thinking, conscious, eternal soul which lives within the body) *will return to God who gave it"* (*Ecclesiastes 12:7*).

b. Why Are We Here?

Life on earth is very short. Death will soon come to each one of us. Therefore, we are not wise if we live only to satisfy the needs of our bodies. We are also very foolish if we live only for the pleasures of this world.

The Apostles John warned: *"Do not love the world or the things in the world. If anyone loves the world, the love of the Father is not in him. For all that is in the world - the lust of the flesh, the lust of the eyes, and the pride of life - is not of the Father but is of the world. And the World is passing away, and the lust of it; but he who does the will of God abides forever"* (*1 John 2:15-17*).

Jesus Christ, the Son of God, asked: *"What is a man profited if he gains the whole world, and loses his own soul? Or what shall a man give in exchange for his soul"* (*Matthew 16:26*)? Our purpose on this earth is to bring glory to God by doing what He has told us to do in the

Bible. A wise man wrote: *"Fear God and keep His commandments, for this is the whole duty of man"* (*Ecclesiastes 12:13*).

c. Where Are We Going?

Where will our spirits go when we die? What happens when we leave this earth? After we die, we will go to be judged by God. *"It is appointed unto men once to die, but after this the judgment"* (*Hebrews 9:27*).

Each person will be judged for his own life (*Romans 14:12*). Each will be judged according to the way they have lived on earth (*2 Corinthians 5:10*).

After the Judgment, there are only two possible places to go. One place is for those who have lived for God and served His son, Jesus Christ. It is a place of peace, happiness, and rest. It is called Heaven (*John14:1-3; 2 Corinthians 4:16 & 5:6; Philippians 3:20; Revelation 21:3-5*). The other place is for those who refuse to obey God, reject Jesus Christ, or spend their lives in the pleasures of this world. It is called *"Hell," "the second death,"* and the *"lake of fire"* (*Matthew 10:28; Matthew 25:41, 46; 2 Thessalonians 1:7-10*).

d. I Must Choose

God loves us and wants us to be saved. He gave His only begotten Son, Jesus Christ, to die as a sacrifice for our sins so that we can be saved (*John 3:16*). But God does not force us to be saved. He wants us to choose for ourselves. Jesus invites us to come to Him: *"Come to Me, all you who labour and are heavy laden, and I will give you rest. Take My yoke upon you and learn from Me, for I am gentle and lowly in heart, and you will find rest for your souls"* (*Matthew 11:28-29*).

In order to come to Jesus, we must:

- believe that He is the Christ, the Son of the living God (***John 8:24***);

- repent of all our past sins (***Luke 13:3***);

- confess our faith in Christ before men (***Romans 10:9-10; Acts 8:37***);

- be buried in water (baptism) and raised up out of the water to live as a new person (***Romans 6:3-5; Acts2:38; 2 Corinthians 5:17***).

CHAPTER 2

GOD

a. GOD

"In the beginning God created the heavens and the earth" (*Genesis 1:1*). This is the first verse in the Bible.

1. All things begin with God.
2. The Bible begins with God.
3. A study of the Bible must also begin with God, for the Bible is God's book.

"What is God like?" "How can we know there is a God?" These are the most important questions anyone can ask. Nothing is of greater importance than the answers to these questions. The answer we give to these questions will determine (decide) how we live on the earth. The answers we give to these questions will determine where we will live after this life on this earth is over. Let us turn to the Bible, God's Book, to learn the answers.

What is God like?

<u>God is eternal!</u> God has always lived. He will always live. The Bible says of God, "**Before the mountains were brought forth, Or ever You had formed the earth and the world, Even from everlasting to everlasting, You are God**" (*Psalm 90:2*).

All people who live on the earth will grow old. All will die. But God can never grow old or die. Let us hear the Bible again: "**You, Lord, in the beginning laid the foundation of the earth, And the heavens are the work of Your hands. They will perish, but You remain; And they will all grow old like a garment; Like a cloak You will fold them up, And they will be changed. But You are the same, And Your years will not fail**" (*Hebrews 1:10-12*).

God is all powerful! "**Is anything too hard for the Lord?**" (**Genesis 18:14**). We human beings are weak. There are many things we do not have the strength to do. But God has all power. He can do anything. By His great power, God created the heavens and the earth. By His great power, God created man. We can trust the promises of God, for He has the power to fulfil them.

God is all-knowing! God knows everything, for God sees everything. It is possible to hide things from the eyes of men, but nothing can be hidden from God. "**For the ways of man are before the eyes of the Lord, And He ponders all his paths**" (*Proverbs 5:21*). "**God is greater than our heart, and knows all things**" (*1 John 3:20*).

God is unchanging! Everything in this world changes. Governments change when nations become independent and new leaders replace old leaders. Ways of living change. Habits and customs of people change. The weather changes. Styles of clothing change. Even our bodies change as we grow older. But God never changes! He is the same yesterday, today, and forever. "**For I am the Lord, I do not change**" (*Malachi 3:6*).

God is spirit! God is not a human being as you and I are. "**God is Spirit, and those who worship Him must worship in spirit and truth**" (*John 4:24*). God does not have weaknesses and sicknesses of the body as you and I do. "**For a spirit does not have flesh and bones as you see I have**" (*Luke 24:39*).

God is light! "**This is the message which we have heard from Him and declare to you, that God is light and in Him is no darkness at all**" (*1 John 1:5*). There is no darkness (sin) in God. Therefore (for this reason) we can trust Him for He will not deceive (lie to or mislead) us.

God is love! "**He who does not love does not know God, for God is love**" (*1 John 4:8*). God loves us. He has proved His great love for us by giving His Son to die for our sins. "**In this is love, not that we loved God but that He loved us and sent His Son to be the propitiation** (to pay the price -- His death on the cross) **for our sins**" (*1 John 4:10*).

God is holy! "**You shall be holy, for I the Lord your God am holy**" (*Leviticus 19:2*).

God is righteous! God cannot do any wrong. He hates all sin. "**For the Lord is righteous, He loves righteousness; His countenance beholds the upright**" (*Psalm 11:7*).

God is merciful! God loves us. Although He hates sin, He is merciful. He will forgive our sins if we truly repent (make up our minds to turn away from practicing sin and turn back to God). "**The Lord is merciful and gracious, Slow to anger, and abounding in mercy**" (*Psalm 103:8*).

How do we know there is a God?

We know there is a God because of the things which He has made. "**The heavens declare the glory of God; And the firmament shows His handiwork**" (*Psalm 19:1*).

When we see a house we know that someone wise enough and strong enough built it. A house cannot exist without a builder. In the same way, when we see the sun, moon, stars, the earth, and all that is in the earth, we know they have a Builder. Someone wise enough and strong enough made all these things. Only God has power to create the heavens and the earth. Therefore, we know there is a God when we see the things He has made.

We know there is a God because our hearts or conscience tell us. People have always believed in a God. This has been true in every country and in every age. People have often had false ideas about God but they have always believed in Him. (*Romans 2:14-16*).

We know there is a God because He has revealed Himself to us in His Son, Jesus Christ. The Bible says: "**God, who at various times and in various ways spoke in time past to the fathers by the prophets, has in these last days spoken to us by His Son, whom He has appointed heir of all things, through whom also He made the worlds**" (*Hebrews 1:1-2*).

b. Authority in Christianity

We must have standards and authorities in all the affairs of life. If we do not, then we have much confusion. Every nation has a government which exercises authority over it. The headmaster and teachers exercise authority in the school. Parents exercise authority in the home.

In Christianity we see much division and confusion. Why? Because we fail to be guided by the true standard of authority! The result is hundreds of churches with many different teachings. Before this confusion can be cleared, we must all agree on an authority in Christianity. What will it be?

The Bible is the inspired Word of God

The Bible is the authority in Christianity because it is the inspired Word of God. The apostle Paul, in writing to Timothy, said:

"All Scripture is given by inspiration of God, and is profitable for doctrine, for reproof, for correction, for instruction in righteousness, that the man of God may be complete, thoroughly equipped for every good work" (2 Timothy 3:16-17).

Peter said, *"Holy men of God spoke as they were moved by the Holy Spirit" (2 Peter 1:21).*

Peter is talking about the men who wrote the Bible. They were men who were told what to write. The Holy Spirit is the one who told them. If we listen to what the Bible says, we are listening to God. God is perfect. What He says is right. Man is not perfect. He makes mistakes. We must not listen to man because he is sometimes wrong. Since God cannot be wrong, we must listen to Him. Then we know we are right.

"Your word is truth" (John 17:17). The Bible is the Word of God. The words of God are truth. Therefore, the Bible contains all truth *(John 16:13).*

Man cannot direct his own way

The Bible is the authority in Christianity because man cannot direct his own way.

"O Lord, I know the way of man is not in himself; It is not in man who walks to direct his own steps" (Jeremiah 10:23).

Many people think that they can decide by themselves what is right in Christianity. When man tries to direct his own way, he finds much trouble. When he listens to God, he does much better. If man were able to direct his own way, God would not have given us the Bible. In order to find the way of life that is pleasing to God, we must let the Bible be our guide.

We will be judged by the Bible

The Bible is the authority in Christianity because we will be judged by it at the second coming of Christ.

"It is appointed for men to die once, but after this the judgment" (**Hebrews 9:27**).

No one can escape death. The whole world agrees with that. Neither can a person escape the judgment. Since we cannot escape the judgment, we must prepare for it. But how can we prepare for it?

By listening to Jesus. God gave Jesus authority to speak. It will be the words of Christ that will judge us. Listen to what Jesus has to say:

"He who rejects Me, and does not receive My words, has that which judges him -- the word that I have spoken will judge him in the last day" (*John 12:48*).

Every man will be judged by his own life.

"Then He will reward each according to his works" (*Matthew 16:27*).

"For we must all appear before the judgment seat of Christ, that each one may receive the things done in the body, according to what he has done, whether good or bad" (*2 Corinthians 5:10*).

The Bible tells us what to do to be saved

The Bible is the authority in Christianity because it tells us what to do to be saved.

"For I am not ashamed of the Gospel of Christ, for it is the power of God to salvation to everyone who believes, for the Jew first and also for the Greek" (Romans 1:16).

"And having been perfected, He became the author of eternal salvation to all who obey Him" (Hebrews 5:9).

No one but Jesus can tell us what to do to be saved. What does Jesus say we must do in order to be saved? Jesus said, *"He who believes and is baptized will be saved; but he who does not believe will be condemned" (Mark 16:16).*

Again we read in the book of Acts:

"Then Peter said to them, Repent, and let every one of you be baptized in the name of Jesus Christ for the remission of sins; and you shall receive the gift of the Holy Spirit" (Acts 2:38).

In order to be saved, we must believe that Jesus is the Son of God and that He died so that we can have forgiveness of sins. We must repent (make up our minds to turn away from practicing sin and turn back to doing things God's way) of our sins. We must confess that Jesus Christ is the Son of God. Then we must be baptized (briefly buried in water) for the forgiveness of our sins.

If we do not accept the Bible as the authority in Christianity, then we are not listening to God. God does not like this. God condemns those who do not listen to Him. Here is what the Bible has to say about it:

"But even if we, or an angel from heaven, preach any other Gospel to you than what we have preached to you, let him be accursed" (Galatians 1:8).

When we listen to men or women, we need to ensure that it is inline with the word of God (scripture), rather than the thoughts of that individual.

"Whoever transgresses and does not abide in the doctrine of Christ does not have God. He who abides in the doctrine of Christ has both the Father (God) *and the Son" (2 John 9).*

Do you listen to the teachings of Christ or to the teachings of men/women?

c. God's Creation

"In the beginning God created the heaven and the earth".

With these words the Bible begins and gives answer to one of life's most important questions. This question is, **"Where did man come from?"** The Bible answers, **"From God."**

THE SIX DAYS OF CREATION

God took only six days to make all that is in the world. These days were 24-hour days each made up of "an evening and a morning." The chart below shows what God made on each day.

FIRST DAY	Light
SECOND DAY	Firmament
THIRD DAY	Dry land and vegetation
FOURTH DAY	Sun, moon and stars
FIFTH DAY	Fish and fowls
SIXTH DAY	Beasts, man and woman

Having finished His creation in six days, the Bible says that on the seventh day God rested.

THE CREATION OF MAN AND WOMAN

The Bible gives the details concerning the creation of man and woman. "**The Lord God formed man of the dust of the ground, and breathed into his nostrils the breath of life,' and man became a living soul.**" He took this man, Adam, and put him into a beautiful garden, called the Garden of Eden. He brought to Adam all the animals and Adam named every one of them.

The Bible then says that God caused Adam to sleep and taking a rib from his side He made a woman from it. Adam called her Eve, for she "was the mother of all the living."

CHAPTER 3

The Downfall of Lucifer/ The Angel of Light

THE DOWNFALL OF LUCIFER, THE ANGEL OF LIGHT

It is important to understand, that God created Lucifer as an Angel of Light, giving him responsibility of all the angles in the heavenly kingdom, being higher and perfect than the other angels; and with such splendour, Lucifer was the most beautiful angel!

However, Lucifer with all the gifts of wisdom and authority given to him by God, corrupted himself and those angels who followed him. **Pride, arrogance, craftiness, and false wisdom was his downfall,** thrown out of heaven by God, and His Angels.

Lucifer's beauty and those of his followers were changed, their appearance from angelic angels into hideous demonic creatures, because of their desire to follow evilness and the lie. Their intent for making the choice of following a lie, removed themselves from heaven, where they were in close proximity with God.

For being unlawful to God, Lucifer was punished to a demonic form, which was greater than those of his followers. God removed/detached all previous angelic responsibilities from Lucifer, changing his name to Satan meaning "adversary, one who withstands". He is also known as Prince of Darkness, Beelzebub, Father of Lies, the Dragon, Mephistopheles, Lord of the Flies, and the Antichrist.

***Revelation 12:7-9* states:**

"(7) And war broke out in heaven: Michal and his angels fought with the dragon; and the dragon and his angels fought, (8) but they did not prevail, nor was a place found for them in heaven any longer. (9) So the great dragon was cast out, that serpent of old, called the Devil and Satan, who deceives the whole world; he was cast to the earth, and his angels were cast out with him".

Ezekiel 28:12-18

12 "Son of man, take up a lamentation for the king of Tyre, and say to him, 'Thus says the Lord God:
"You *were* the seal of perfection,
Full of wisdom and perfect in beauty.

13 You were in Eden, the garden of God;
Every precious stone *was* your covering:
The sardius, topaz, and diamond,
Beryl, onyx, and jasper,
Sapphire, turquoise, and emerald with gold.
The workmanship of your timbrels and pipes
Was prepared for you on the day you were created.

14 "You *were* the anointed cherub who covers;
I established you;
You were on the holy mountain of God;
You walked back and forth in the midst of fiery stones.

15 You *were* perfect in your ways from the day you were created,
Till iniquity was found in you.

16 "By the abundance of your trading
You became filled with violence within,

And you sinned;
Therefore I cast you as a profane thing
Out of the mountain of God;
And I destroyed you, O covering cherub,
From the midst of the fiery stones.

17 "Your heart was lifted up because of your beauty;
You corrupted your wisdom for the sake of your splendour;
I cast you to the ground,
I laid you before kings,
That they might gaze at you.

18 "You defiled your sanctuaries
By the multitude of your iniquities,
By the iniquity of your trading;
Therefore I brought fire from your midst;
It devoured you,
And I turned you to ashes upon the earth
In the sight of all who saw you.

Isaiah 14:12-20

12 "How you are fallen from heaven,
O Lucifer, son of the morning!
How you are cut down to the ground,
You who weakened the nations!

13 For you have said in your heart:
'I will ascend into heaven,
I will exalt my throne above the stars of God;
I will also sit on the mount of the congregation
On the farthest sides of the north;

14 I will ascend above the heights of the clouds,
I will be like the Most High.'

15 Yet you shall be brought down to Sheol,
To the lowest depths of the Pit.

16 "Those who see you will gaze at you,
And consider you, saying:
'Is this the man who made the earth tremble,
Who shook kingdoms,

17 Who made the world as a wilderness
And destroyed its cities,
Who did not open the house of his prisoners?'

18 "All the kings of the nations,
All of them, sleep in glory,
Everyone in his own house;

19 But you are cast out of your grave
Like an abominable branch,
Like the garment of those who are slain,
Thrust through with a sword,
Who go down to the stones of the pit,
Like a corpse trodden underfoot.

20 You will not be joined with them in burial,
Because you have destroyed your land
And slain your people.
The brood of evildoers shall never be named.

New Testament

Matthew 24:24

For false christ's and false prophets will rise and show great signs and wonders to deceive, if possible, even the elect.

John 8:43-45
Why do you not understand My speech? Because you are not able to listen to My word. You are of your father the devil, and the desires of your father you want to do. He was a murderer from the beginning, and does not stand in the truth, because there is no truth in him. When he speaks a lie, he speaks from his own resources, for he is a liar and the father of it. But because I tell the truth, you do not believe Me.

John 8:47
He who is of God hears God's words; therefore you do not hear, because you are not of God."

John 17:14
I have given them Your word; and the world has hated them because they are not of the world, just as I am not of the world.

Ephesians 2:1-3
And you He made alive, who were dead in trespasses and sins, in which you once walked according to the course of this world, according to the prince of the power of the air, the spirit who now works in the sons of disobedience, among whom also we all once conducted ourselves in the lusts of our flesh, fulfilling the desires of the flesh and of the mind, and were by nature children of wrath, just as the others.

Ephesians 6:11-12
Put on the whole armour of God, that you may be able to stand against the wiles of the devil. For we do not wrestle against flesh and blood, but against principalities, against powers, against the rulers of the darkness of this age, against spiritual hosts of wickedness in the heavenly places.

2 Corinthians 11:3-4
But I fear, lest somehow, as the serpent deceived Eve by his craftiness, so your minds may be corrupted from the simplicity that is in Christ. For if he who comes preaches another Jesus whom we have not preached, or if you receive a different spirit which you have not received, or a different gospel which you have not accepted 'you may well put up with it!

2 Corinthians 11:14
And no wonder! For Satan himself transforms himself into an angel of light.

1 John 5:18-19
We know that whoever is born of God does not sin; but he who has been born of God keeps himself, and the wicked one does not touch him. We know that we are of God, and the whole world lies under the sway of the wicked one.

2 Thessalonians 2:3
Let no one deceive you by any means; for that Day will not come unless the falling away comes first, and the man of sin is revealed, the son of perdition.

2 Thessalonians 2:6-7
And now you know what is restraining, that he may be revealed in his own time. For the mystery of lawlessness is already at work; only He who now restrains will do so until He is taken out of the way.

2 Thessalonians 2:10
and with all unrighteous deception among those who perish, because they did not receive the love of the truth, that they might be saved.

James 3:15-16
This wisdom does not descend from above, but is earthly, sensual, demonic. For where envy and self-seeking exist, confusion and every evil thing are there.

1 Peter 5:6
Therefore, humble yourselves under the mighty hand of God, that He may exalt you in due time.

1 Peter 5:8-9
Be sober, be vigilant; because your adversary the devil walks about like a roaring lion, seeking whom he may devour. Resist him, steadfast in the faith, knowing that the same sufferings are experienced by your brotherhood in the world.

Revelation 12:4
His tail drew a third of the stars of heaven and threw them to the earth. And the dragon stood before the woman who was ready to give birth, to devour her Child as soon as it was born.

Revelation 12:12
Therefore rejoice, O heavens, and you who dwell in them! Woe to the inhabitants of the earth and the sea! For the devil has come down to you, having great wrath, because he knows that he has a short time.

CHAPTER 4

The Old Testament

a. The Old Testament

The Bible has two main divisions.

The first division is called the Old Testament. The second division is called the New Testament.

The Old Testament includes the first 39 books of the Bible. It begins with Genesis and ends with the book of Malachi.

The Old Testament tells the story of God's dealings (working) with mankind from the beginning of the world until the birth of Jesus. Although we are not governed by the Old Testament today, it still has relevance and must be studied. (***Romans 15:4***) and (***1 Corinthians 10:11***).

The writings of the Old Testament

The Old Testament was first written in the Hebrew language. The 39 books of the Old Testament were written by several different men.

These men received the message which they wrote from God. In the New Testament, we learn how these writers received the message they wrote: **"for prophecy never came by the will of man, but holy men of God spoke as they were moved by the Holy Spirit"** (*2 Peter 1:21*).

The divisions of the Old Testament

We have learned that the Bible has two major divisions, the Old Testament and the New Testament. The Old Testament can be further divided into four main sections. These sections are: Law, History, Poetry, and Prophecy.

b. The books of the Law, History, Poetry and Prophecy

The books of the Law

The first 5 books of the Old Testament make up the first section of Law. The books in this section are **Genesis, Exodus, Leviticus, Numbers,** and **Deuteronomy.** These books were written by Moses, the great servant of God.

Genesis is the story of the beginning of all things. In Genesis we learn about the beginning of man and woman, marriage, sin, death, different languages, the nation of Israel, and God's plan to save man from his sins.

Genesis also talks about men such as Noah, Abraham, Isaac, Jacob, and Joseph. These men are often called Patriarchs. The word "patriarch" means "a father," or a "head of a family." The book of Genesis tells us about the Patriarchal Age (from Adam and Eve to Moses' receiving the Ten Commandment Law on Mount Sinai).

In the Patriarchal Age the people did not have God's commandments written down in the Bible. Instead, God spoke directly to the patriarchs and revealed His commandments and teachings to them.

Exodus tells about the nation of Israel. God had chosen Israel to be His special people. From Israel God planned later to bring Jesus to be the Saviour of the world. The people of Israel had gone to live in Egypt during a time of famine (no food). The Egyptians made slaves of them. Exodus tells the story of how God sent Moses to lead the people of Israel out of Egypt.

Leviticus and Deuteronomy contain the first written law which God gave to mankind. This law was given to Moses on Mount Sinai. It contains the Ten Commandments and many other laws. This law of Moses was given ONLY to the nation of Israel (*Exodus 19:3; Deuteronomy 5:1*).

It was to last until the death of Christ on the cross. Christ fulfilled the law of Moses and took it out of the way. Read *Matthew 5:17-18; Galatians 3:23-28; Colossians 2:13-14*.

Numbers is a book of history and also contains some of the laws which God gave to Israel. It tells about Israel's wanderings in the desert for forty years before they entered the land of Canaan.

The books of history

The second section of the Old Testament is called History. This section contains twelve books. They are **Joshua, Judges, Ruth, 1 and 2 Samuel, 1 and 2 Kings, 1 and 2 Chronicles, Ezra, Nehemiah, and Esther.**

These twelve books tell the history of the nation of Israel. They tell about the wars in which God helped Israel destroy the wicked people of Canaan. They tell about the building of God's temple in Jerusalem. They tell how Israel became a rich, powerful nation but later divided into two separate kingdoms called Judah and Israel.

These books also tell how the people of Israel forgot about their God and worshipped idols (false gods). God punished them for their sins by permitting other nations to make slaves of them. But whenever Israel repented (decided to stop doing wrong things and turn back to God, doing things God's way), God permitted them to return to their home.

The books of poetry

There are five books in this section.

They are **Job, Psalms, Proverbs, Ecclesiastes, and Song of Solomon.**

Job is the story of a man who suffered much. Even though he had many troubles, he still remained faithful to God. Psalms are poems and songs written by King David and others. These poems praise God for His goodness, power, and glory. Proverbs is a book of wise sayings. It was written by King Solomon and others.

Ecclesiastes was written by King Solomon. It tells about a man who tried to find happiness in riches, love, power, fame, and learning. He found that none of these could bring true happiness. He learned that true happiness can only come from fearing God and keeping His commandments. The Song of Solomon is a love song.

The books of prophecy

The last section of the Old Testament is Prophecy. It contains seventeen books. These books were written by the great prophets of God whose names they bear. They are **Isaiah, Jeremiah, Lamentations, Ezekiel, Daniel, Hosea, Joel, Amos, Obadiah, Jonah, Micah, Nahum, Habakkuk, Zephaniah, Haggai, Zechariah,** and **Malachi.**

These prophets were men who spoke for God. The prophets had big jobs to do. First: They rebuked the people of their own time for their sins. Second: They were permitted by God to see into the future. God gave them the power to foretell things which would happen many years later. For example, the prophet Isaiah lived 700 years before Christ came to the earth. Yet, he (Isaiah) foretold many things about Christ and His kingdom. Chapter 53, which tells of Christ's death for our sins

c. The Fall of Mankind and Why?

NJKV Bible *Genesis 1-4.*

When God placed man in the Garden of Eden, he told him that he could eat of every tree in the garden, except one called the "tree of the knowledge of good and evil." If he did, God said, "You will die the very day you eat of it." The Bible tells of the coming of the Devil in the form of a serpent and persuading Eve to eat of that tree. She then persuaded Adam to eat of it.

Because of their sin (disobeying God) they were driven Out of the garden: they were separated from God--they were dead spiritually. Today when we disobey God we die spiritually--we are separated from Him. As further punishment, God told Eve she would have pain in bearing children, man would have to work hard to get food, the serpent would have to crawl upon his belly and the Devil was told that someday he would be crushed. (**Genesis 3:14-19; Romans 16:20**).

Adam and Eve had two boys, Cain and Abel. When God told these boys to offer sacrifices, Abel did just what God said, but Cain offered something other than what God had said. (Note: This is sin, whenever one disobeys God, it is wrong). When God accepted Abel's sacrifice, Cain became angry and killed his brother. Later Adam and Eve had other children. One of these, named "Seth." is the one through whom Jesus was to come later on.

d. Sin, what changed?

John says ". . . sin is lawlessness" [breaking the law] (NKJV Bible *1 John 3:4*). Again, he says that "All unrighteousness is sin . . ." (NKJV Bible *1 John 5:17*).

Every nation has laws. When a person **does not obey** these laws, he has done wrong. God has laws which we are to obey. These laws are found in the Bible. When we do not obey God's law, we sin. All grown people have sinned. "**For all have sinned and fall short of the glory of God**" (NKJV Bible *Romans 3:23*).

We must always look out for sin. Sin is deceitful.

"But exhort one another daily, while it is called 'Today,' lest any of you be hardened through the deceitfulness of sin" (NKJV Bible *Hebrews 3:13*).

God hates sin. Let us, therefore, not be deceived by it.

The Cause of Sin

All things in life have a cause. We sleep because we are tired. We eat because we are hungry. No matter what we do in life there is a cause for it. This is also true with sin. Desiring something we should not have may lead to sin. "**But each one is tempted when he is drawn away by his own desires and enticed. Then, when desire has conceived, it gives birth to sin; and sin, when it is full-grown, brings forth death**" (*James 1:14- 15*).

The cause of sin is lust [desire]. If we do away with these wrong desires, then we will not sin.

Different Ways We Sin

There are two ways that we can sin.

First, by doing that which we are not supposed to do. A father once told his son not to swim in a river. The son went and swam in the river. The son did not obey his father. He did that which he was not supposed to do. God has told us what we are **not** to do.

Now the works of the flesh are evident, which are: "**adultery, fornication, uncleanness, lewdness [thinking and practicing immoral things], idolatry, sorcery, hatred, contentions, jealousies, outbursts of wrath, selfish ambitions, dissensions, heresies, envy, murders, drunkenness, revelries, and the like; of which I tell you beforehand, just as I also told you in time past, that those who practice such things will not inherit the kingdom of God**" (*Galatians 5:19-21*).

When we do these things, we have sinned. We have done that which God told us not to do.

Second, we sin by not doing that which we are supposed to do. A mother told her daughter to wash the dishes. The daughter did not wash the dishes. She did wrong. She did not do what her mother had told her to do. God has told us what to do to be pleasing to Him. It is all written in the Bible. When we do not do what God says to do, then we are guilty of sin. For example, God has told us to worship Him on Sunday, the first day of the week. "**Not forsaking the assembling of ourselves together, as is the manner of some, but exhorting one another, and so much the more as you see the Day approaching**" (*Hebrews 10:25*).

When we do not worship God on Sunday, we sin. There are many other commands that God has given for us to do. **We must read the**

New Testament to learn what they are. Then we must do them. <u>If we do not do them, then we are guilty of sin.</u>

Results of Sin

Earlier we learned about a girl who did not obey her mother when she was told to wash the dishes. Now what does the mother do with such a girl? She must punish her. Why? Because the daughter must learn to do what she is told to do. If the girl is not punished, then the next time she is told to do something, she won't do it. God will also punish those who do not obey Him.

"In flaming fire <u>taking vengeance</u> on [punishing] those who do not know God, and on those who do not obey the gospel of our Lord Jesus Christ" (*2 Thessalonians 1:8*). We do not have to receive this punishment. God has provided a way for us to be forgiven of our sins. Jesus Christ is the way to God.

"Jesus said to him, "I am the way, the truth, and the life. No one comes to the Father except through Me" (*John 14:6*). Since Jesus is the Way, we must listen to Him. Here is what He says about salvation: "He who believes and is baptized will be saved; but he who does not believe will be condemned" (*Mark 16:16*).

Therefore, we must believe in Jesus Christ as the Son of God. We must repent of our sins. Then we must be baptized in the name of Jesus Christ for the forgiveness of our sins. If we do this, we will be obeying God. He then will not punish us forever and ever. **Have you obeyed God and done what He says to do to have the forgiveness of your sins?**

e. God's Commandments, Judgements and Laws

God's commandments, judgements and laws were written as an instruction on how every man, woman and child should behave in this world (regardless of nationality, race, ethnicity, whether you are Royalty, rich, poor or slave).

Such laws clearly illustrate God's love for every human, for mankind was created by God, in his likeness, with freewill (before falling to sin). This is illustrated in the following:

Genesis, 1:26-31
26 Then God said, "Let Us make man in Our image, according to Our likeness; let them have dominion over the fish of the sea, over the birds of the air, and over the cattle, over all the earth and over every creeping thing that creeps on the earth." 27 So God created man in His *own* image; in the image of God He created him; male and female He created them. 28 Then God blessed them, and God said to them, "Be fruitful and multiply; fill the earth and subdue it; have dominion over the fish of the sea, over the birds of the air, and over every living thing that moves on the earth."

29 And God said, "See, I have given you every herb *that* yields seed which *is* on the face of all the earth, and every tree whose fruit yields seed; to you it shall be for food. 30 Also, to every beast of the earth, to every bird of the air, and to everything that creeps on the earth, in which *there is* life, *I have given* every green herb for food"; and it was so. 31 Then God saw everything that He had made, and indeed *it was* very good. So the evening and the morning were the sixth day.

Genesis, 2:7
7 And the Lord God formed man *of* the dust of the ground, and breathed into his nostrils the breath of life; and man became a living being.

Psalm 139:14
14 I will praise You, for I am fearfully *and* wonderfully made;

Marvelous are Your works,

And *that* my soul knows very well.

Psalm 82:6
6 I said, "You *are* gods,

And all of you *are* children of the Most High.

John 10:34-36
34 Jesus answered them, "Is it not written in your law, *I said, "You are gods*?

35 If He called them gods, to whom the word of God came (and the Scripture cannot be broken),

36 do you say of Him whom the Father sanctified and sent into the world, 'You are blaspheming,' jbecause I said, 'I am the Son of God'?

Since the very beginning, when Adam and Eve sinned against God in the Garden of Eden (***Genesis Chapters, 2-3*** - through listening and obeying the lie of Satan (serpent), instead of adhering to God's instruction "not to eat of the tree of the knowledge of good and evil you shall not eat, for in the day that you eat of it you shall surely die"), that sin infected the world by the choice that mankind made by disobeying God.

However, God had a plan for the world, to save it from sin and everlasting death, through believing on Jesus Christ His Son, our Saviour, and Redeemer of all Sins, and through following God's Commandments, Judgements and Laws.

Genesis 3:15
15 And I will put enmity
Between you and the woman,
And between your seed and her Seed;
He shall bruise your head,
And you shall bruise His heel."

Malachi 3:1-6
The Coming Messenger
3 "Behold, I send My messenger,
And he will prepare the way before Me.
And the Lord, whom you seek,
Will suddenly come to His temple,
Even the Messenger of the covenant,
In whom you delight.
Behold, He is coming,"
Says the Lord of hosts.

2 "But who can endure the day of His coming?
And who can stand when He appears?
For He *is* like a refiner's fire
And like launderers' soap.

3 He will sit as a refiner and a purifier of silver;
He will purify the sons of Levi,
And purge them as gold and silver,
That they may offer to the Lord
An offering in righteousness.

4 "Then the offering of Judah and Jerusalem
Will be pleasant to the Lord,
As in the days of old,
As in former years.

5 And I will come near you for judgment;
I will be a swift witness
Against sorcerers,
Against adulterers,
Against perjurers,
Against those who exploit wage earners and widows and orphans,
And against those who turn away an alien—
Because they do not fear Me,"
Says the Lord of hosts.

6 "For I *am* the Lord, I do not change;
Therefore you are not consumed, O sons of Jacob.
7 Yet from the days of your fathers
You have gone away from My ordinances
And have not kept *them*.
Return to Me, and I will return to you,"
Says the Lord of hosts.
"But you said,
'In what way shall we return?'

To enable the reader to have context of God's commandments, judgements, and laws, including those listed abominations, I have provided an illustration of passage references from the Holy Bible, to enable readers to examine using their Bibles.

f. The Ten Commandments
(God's laws Old and New Testaments)

Exodus, Chapter 20:1-17

20 And God spoke all these words:

2 "I am the Lord your God, who brought you out of Egypt, out of the land of slavery.

3 "You shall have no other gods before me.

4 "You shall not make for yourself an image in the form of anything in heaven above or on the earth beneath or in the waters below.

5 You shall not bow down to them or worship them; for I, the Lord your God, am a jealous God, punishing the children for the sin of the parents to the third and fourth generation of those who hate me,

6 but showing love to a thousand generations of those who love me and keep my commandments.

7 "You shall not misuse the name of the Lord your God, for the Lord will not hold anyone guiltless who misuses his name.

8 "Remember the Sabbath day by keeping it holy.

9 Six days you shall labour and do all your work,

10 but the seventh day is a sabbath to the Lord your God. On it you shall not do any work, neither you, nor your son or daughter, nor your male or female servant, nor your animals, nor any foreigner residing in your towns.

11 For in six days the Lord made the heavens and the earth, the sea, and all that is in them, but he rested on the seventh day. Therefore the Lord blessed the Sabbath day and made it holy.

12 "Honour your father and your mother, so that you may live long in the land the Lord your God is giving you.

13 "You shall not murder.

14 "You shall not commit adultery.

15 "You shall not steal.

16 "You shall not give false testimony against your neighbour.

17 "You shall not covet your neighbour's house. You shall not covet your neighbour's wife, or his male or female servant, his ox or donkey, or anything that belongs to your neighbour."

g. Bible verses about Judgement

	Righteousness	Neighbour	
Therefore you are inexcusable, O man, whoever you are who judge, for in whatever you judge another you condemn yourself; for you who judge practice the same things. **Romans 2:1**			
Judge not, that you be not judged. **Matthew 7:1**	Law		
Every way of a man is right in his own eyes, But the Lord weighs the hearts. **Proverbs 21:2**	Righteousness	Understanding	Thoughts
Therefore let us not judge one another anymore, but rather resolve this, not to put a stumbling block or a cause to fall in our brother's way. **Romans 14:13**	Gentleness	Neighbour	

	Speaking	Sin	Forgiveness	Faith	Equipment
But I say to you that for every idle word men may speak, they will give account of it in the day of judgment. **Matthew 12:36**					
And why do you look at the speck in your brother's eye, but do not consider the plank in your own eye? **Matthew 7:3**					
Judge not, and you shall not be judged. Condemn not, and you shall not be condemned. Forgive, and you will be forgiven. **Luke 6:37**					
Who are you to judge another's servant? To his own master he stands or falls. Indeed, he will be made to stand, for God is able to make him stand. **Romans 14:4**					

	Righteousness	Protection	Idols
"No weapon formed against you shall prosper, And every tongue which rises against you in judgment You shall condemn. This is the heritage of the servants of the Lord, And their righteousness is from Me," Says the Lord. **Isaiah 54:17**			
There is one Lawgiver, who is able to save and to destroy. Who are you to judge another? **James 4:12**	Law	Salvation	Neighbour
For as many as have sinned without law will also perish without law, and as many as have sinned in the law will be judged by the law. **Romans 2:12**	Sin	Law	Punishment

Marriage	Desires		
Salvation	Jesus	World	
Food	Sabbath	Jesus	
Marriage is honourable among all, and the bed undefiled; but fornicators and adulterers God will judge. **Hebrews 13:4**			
For God did not send His Son into the world to condemn the world, but that the world through Him might be saved. **John 3:17**			
So let no one judge you in food or in drink, or regarding a festival or a new moon or sabbaths, which are a shadow of things to come, but the substance is of Christ. **Colossians 2:16-17**			

God's Promises Fulfilled: The End Times Prophecy

	Resurrection			
	And I saw the dead, small and great, standing before God, and books were opened. And another book was opened, which is the Book of Life. And the dead were judged according to their works, by the things which were written in the books. The sea gave up the dead who were in it, and Death and Hades delivered up the dead who were in them. And they were judged, each one according to his works. **Revelation 20:12-13**	Food		
		Let not him who eats despise him who does not eat, and let not him who does not eat judge him who eats; for God has received him. **Romans 14:3**	Law	Redeemer	Punishment
			There is therefore now no condemnation to those who are in Christ Jesus, who do not walk according to the flesh, but according to the Spirit. For the law of the Spirit of life in Christ Jesus has made me free from the law of sin and death. **Romans 8:1-2**		

	Self-control	Body			Reward
	Faith				
	Righteousness	Learning			
	Sin		Eternal life		

But I discipline my body and bring it into subjection, lest, when I have preached to others, I myself should become disqualified. **1 Corinthians 9:27**					
He who believes in Him is not condemned; but he who does not believe is condemned already, because he has not believed in the name of the only begotten Son of God. **John 3:18**					
With my soul I have desired You in the night, Yes, by my spirit within me I will seek You early; For when Your judgments are in the earth, The inhabitants of the world will learn righteousness. **Isaiah 26:9**					
For the wages of sin is death, but the gift of God is eternal life in Christ Jesus our Lord. **Romans 6:23**					

But above all, my brethren, do not swear, either by heaven or by earth or with any other oath. But let your "Yes" be "Yes," and your "No," "No," lest you fall into judgment. **James 5:12**	Honesty	Truth	Speaking
He who believes and is baptized will be saved; but he who does not believe will be condemned. **Mark 16:16**	Faith	Salvation	Baptism
Then the Lord knows how to deliver the godly out of temptations and to reserve the unjust under punishment for the day of judgment. **2 Peter 2:9**	Temptation	Punishment	Salvation
I have fought the good fight, I have finished the race, I have kept the faith. Finally, there is laid up for me the crown of righteousness, which the Lord, the righteous Judge, will give to me on that Day, and not to me only but also to all who have loved His appearing. **2 Timothy 4:7-8**	Faith	Righteousness	Reward

h. God laws and abomination

An abomination, as mentioned in the Bible, is a violation of God's law and the tenets of Christianity.

1. God's laws during the time of the Old Testament, relating to the Israelite (Jewish people) nation.

Most Relevant Verses
Leviticus 7:18
So if any of the flesh of the sacrifice of his peace offerings should ever be eaten on the third day, he who offers it will not be accepted, and it will not be reckoned to his benefit. It shall be an offensive thing, and the person who eats of it will bear his own iniquity.
Daniel 11:31
Forces from him will arise, desecrate the sanctuary fortress, and do away with the regular sacrifice. And they will set up the abomination of desolation.
Deuteronomy 17:1
"You shall not sacrifice to the Lord your God an ox or a sheep which has a blemish or any defect, for that is a detestable thing to the Lord your God.
1 Kings 11:5

For Solomon went after Ashtoreth the goddess of the Sidonians and after Milcom the detestable idol of the Ammonites.

Genesis 43:32

So they served him by himself, and them by themselves, and the Egyptians who ate with him by themselves, because the Egyptians could not eat bread with the Hebrews, for that is loathsome to the Egyptians.

Leviticus 19:27

You shall not round off the side-growth of your heads nor harm the edges of your beard.

Genesis 46:34

you shall say, 'Your servants have been keepers of livestock from our youth even until now, both we and our fathers,' that you may live in the land of Goshen; for every shepherd is loathsome to the Egyptians."

Isaiah 1:13

"Bring your worthless offerings no longer,

Incense is an abomination to Me.

New moon and sabbath, the calling of assemblies—

I cannot endure iniquity and the solemn assembly.

Leviticus 7:21

When anyone touches anything unclean, whether human uncleanness, or an unclean animal, or any unclean detestable thing, and eats of the flesh of the sacrifice of peace offerings which belong to the Lord, that person shall be cut off from his people.'"

Deuteronomy 23:18
You shall not bring the hire of a harlot or the wages of a dog into the house of the Lord your God for any votive offering, for both of these are an abomination to the Lord your God.

1 Kings 14:24
There were also male cult prostitutes in the land. They did according to all the abominations of the nations which the Lord dispossessed before the sons of Israel.

Isaiah 66:17
"Those who sanctify and purify themselves to go to the gardens,
Following one in the center,
Who eat swine's flesh, detestable things and mice,
Will come to an end altogether," declares the Lord.

2 Kings 23:13

The high places which were before Jerusalem, which were on the right of the mount of destruction which Solomon the king of Israel had built for Ashtoreth the abomination of the Sidonians, and for Chemosh the abomination of Moab, and for Milcom the abomination of the sons of Ammon, the king defiled.
Isaiah 44:19
No one recalls, nor is there knowledge or understanding to say, "I have burned half of it in the fire and also have baked bread over its coals. I roast meat and eat it. Then I make the rest of it into an abomination, I fall down before a block of wood!"
Jeremiah 32:35
They built the high places of Baal that are in the valley of Ben-hinnom to cause their sons and their daughters to pass through the fire to Molech, which I had not commanded them nor had it entered My mind that they should do this abomination, to cause Judah to sin.
Exodus 10:2
and that you may tell in the hearing of your son, and of your grandson, how I made a mockery of the Egyptians and how I performed My signs among them, that you may know that I am the Lord."
Exodus 8:26
But Moses said, "It is not right to do so, for we will sacrifice to the Lord our God what is an abomination to the Egyptians. If we sacrifice what is an abomination to the Egyptians before their eyes, will they not then stone us?

Jeremiah 6:15

"Were they ashamed because of the abomination they have done?

They were not even ashamed at all;

They did not even know how to blush.

Therefore they shall fall among those who fall;

At the time that I punish them,

They shall be cast down," says the Lord.

Exodus 8:22

But on that day I will set apart the land of Goshen, where My people are living, so that no swarms of flies will be there, in order that you may know that I, the Lord, am in the midst of the land.

Exodus 21:7

"If a man sells his daughter as a female slave, she is not to go free as the male slaves do.

2. God's laws still relevant in the Old and New Testaments

Most Relevant Verses
Leviticus 18:22
You shall not lie with a male as one lies with a female; it is an abomination.
Leviticus 20:13
If there is a man who lies with a male as those who lie with a woman, both of them have committed a detestable act; they shall surely be put to death. Their blood guiltiness is upon them.
Romans 1:18-32   ***The Guilt of Mankind***   [18] For the wrath of God is revealed from heaven against all ungodliness and unrighteousness of men, who suppress the truth in unrighteousness, [19] because what may be known of God is manifest in them, for God has shown it to them. [20] For since the creation of the world His invisible attributes are clearly seen, being understood by the things that are made, even His eternal power and Godhead, so that they are without excuse, [21] because, although they knew God, they did not glorify Him as God, nor were thankful, but became futile in their thoughts, and their foolish hearts were darkened. [22] Professing to be wise, they became fools, [23] and changed the glory of the incorruptible God into an image made like corruptible

man--and birds and four-footed animals and creeping things. 24 Therefore God also gave them up to uncleanness, in the lusts of their hearts, to dishonour their bodies among themselves; 25 who exchanged the truth of God for the lie, and worshiped and served the creature rather than the Creator, who is blessed forever. Amen. 26 For this reason God gave them up to vile passions. For even their women exchanged the natural use for what is against nature. 27 Likewise also the men, leaving the natural use of the woman, burned in their lust for one another, men with men committing what is shameful, and receiving in themselves the penalty of their error which was due. 28 And even as they did not like to retain God in their knowledge, God gave them over to a debased mind, to do those things which are not fitting; 29 being filled with all unrighteousness, sexual immorality, wickedness, covetousness, maliciousness; full of envy, murder, strife, deceit, evil-mindedness; they are whisperers, 30 backbiters, haters of God, violent, proud, boasters, inventors of evil things, disobedient to parents, 31 undiscerning, untrustworthy, unloving, unforgiving, unmerciful; 32 who, knowing the righteous judgment of God, that those who practice such things are deserving of death, not only do the same but also approve of those who practice them.

Deuteronomy 22:5

5A woman shall not wear anything that pertains to a man, nor shall a man put on a woman's garment, for all who do so are an abomination to the Lord your God.

Proverbs 6:16-19

There are six things which the Lord hates,
Yes, seven which are an abomination to Him:
Haughty eyes, a lying tongue,
And hands that shed innocent blood,

A heart that devises wicked plans,
Feet that run rapidly to evil,
A false witness who utters lies,
And one who spreads strife among brothers.
Luke 16:15
And He said to them, "You are those who justify yourselves in the sight of men, but God knows your hearts; for that which is highly esteemed among men is detestable in the sight of God.
Revelation 21:27
and nothing unclean, and no one who practices abomination and lying, shall ever come into it, but only those whose names are written in the Lamb's book of life.
Proverbs 12:22
Lying lips are an abomination to the Lord,
But those who deal faithfully are His delight.
Deuteronomy 7:25

The graven images of their gods you are to burn with fire; you shall not covet the silver or the gold that is on them, nor take it for yourselves, or you will be snared by it, for it is an abomination to the Lord your God.

Proverbs 11:1
A false balance is an abomination to the Lord,
But a just weight is His delight.

Daniel 12:11
From the time that the regular sacrifice is abolished and the abomination of desolation is set up, there will be 1,290 days.

Daniel 9:27
And he will make a firm covenant with the many for one week, but in the middle of the week he will put a stop to sacrifice and grain offering; and on the wing of abominations will come one who makes desolate, even until a complete destruction, one that is decreed, is poured out on the one who makes desolate."

Proverbs 13:19
Desire realized is sweet to the soul,
But it is an abomination to fools to turn away from evil.

Matthew 24:15
"Therefore when you see the abomination of desolation which was spoken of through Daniel the prophet, standing in the holy place (let the reader understand)".

Mark 13:14
"But when you see the abomination of desolation standing where it should not be (let the reader understand), then those who are in Judea must flee to the mountains.

Proverbs 29:27
An unjust man is abominable to the righteous,
And he who is upright in the way is abominable to the wicked.

Leviticus 11:20
'All the winged insects that walk on all fours are detestable to you.

Leviticus 11:23
But all other winged insects which are four-footed are detestable to you.

Leviticus 11:41
'Now every swarming thing that swarms on the earth is detestable, not to be eaten.

Leviticus 11:42

Whatever crawls on its belly, and whatever walks on all fours, whatever has many feet, in respect to every swarming thing that swarms on the earth, you shall not eat them, for they are detestable.

Deuteronomy 27:15

'Cursed is the man who makes an idol or a molten image, an abomination to the Lord, the work of the hands of the craftsman, and sets it up in secret.' And all the people shall answer and say, 'Amen.'

Proverbs 15:8

The sacrifice of the wicked is an abomination to the Lord,
But the prayer of the upright is His delight.

Ezekiel 22:11

One has committed abomination with his neighbour's wife and another has lewdly defiled his daughter-in-law. And another in you has humbled his sister, his father's daughter.

Proverbs 3:32

For the devious are an abomination to the Lord;

But He is intimate with the upright.
Proverbs 11:20
The perverse in heart are an abomination to the Lord, But the blameless in their walk are His delight.
Deuteronomy 22:23-24
"If there is a girl who is a virgin engaged to a man, and another man finds her in the city and lies with her, then you shall bring them both out to the gate of that city and you shall stone them to death; the girl, because she did not cry out in the city, and the man, because he has violated his neighbour's wife. Thus you shall purge the evil from among you.
Deuteronomy 12:31
You shall not behave thus toward the Lord your God, for every abominable act which the Lord hates they have done for their gods; for they even burn their sons and daughters in the fire to their gods.
Leviticus 11:13
'These, moreover, you shall detest among the birds; they are abhorrent, not to be eaten: the eagle and the vulture and the buzzard.

Proverbs 16:5	
Everyone who is proud in heart is an abomination to the Lord; Assuredly, he will not be unpunished.	
Mark 7:20-23	
And He was saying, "That which proceeds out of the man, that is what defiles the man. For from within, out of the heart of men, proceed the evil thoughts, fornications, thefts, murders, adulteries, deeds of coveting and wickedness, as well as deceit, sensuality, envy, slander, pride and foolishness.	
Deuteronomy 24:1-4	
"When a man takes a wife and marries her, and it happens that she finds no favour in his eyes because he has found some indecency in her, and he writes her a certificate of divorce and puts it in her hand and sends her out from his house, and she leaves his house and goes and becomes another man's wife, and if the latter husband turns against her and writes her a certificate of divorce and puts it in her hand and sends her out of his house, or if the latter husband dies who took her to be his wife (read more).	
Deuteronomy 25:13-16	
"You shall not have in your bag differing weights, a large and a small. You shall not have in your house differing measures, a large and a small. You shall have a full and just weight; you shall have a full and just measure, that your days may be prolonged in the land which the Lord your God gives you (read more).	

Proverbs 20:10
Differing weights and differing measures,
Both of them are abominable to the Lord.

Leviticus 11:12
Whatever in the water does not have fins and scales is abhorrent to you.

Leviticus 20:14
If there is a man who marries a woman and her mother, it is immorality; both he and they shall be burned with fire, so that there will be no immorality in your midst.

Revelation 21:8
But for the cowardly and unbelieving and abominable and murderers and immoral persons and sorcerers and idolaters and all liars, their part will be in the lake that burns with fire and brimstone, which is the second death."

Deuteronomy 7:25-26

The graven images of their gods you are to burn with fire; you shall not covet the silver or the gold that is on them, nor take it for yourselves, or you will be snared by it, for it is an abomination to the Lord your God. You shall not bring an abomination into your house, and like it come under the ban; you shall utterly detest it and you shall utterly abhor it, for it is something banned.

Leviticus 18:29

For whoever does any of these abominations, those persons who do so shall be cut off from among their people.

Deuteronomy 25:16

For everyone who does these things, everyone who acts unjustly is an abomination to the Lord your God.

Proverbs 6:16

There are six things which the Lord hates,
Yes, seven which are an abomination to Him:

Proverbs 24:9

The devising of folly is sin,
And the scoffer is an abomination to men.

Proverbs 17:15	
	He who justifies the wicked and he who condemns the righteous,
	Both of them alike are an abomination to the Lord.
Leviticus 11:10-12	
	But whatever is in the seas and in the rivers that does not have fins and scales among all the teeming life of the water, and among all the living creatures that are in the water, they are detestable things to you, and they shall be abhorrent to you; you may not eat of their flesh, and their carcasses you shall detest. Whatever in the water does not have fins and scales is abhorrent to you.
Leviticus 11:11	
	and they shall be abhorrent to you; you may not eat of their flesh, and their carcasses you shall detest.
Deuteronomy 7:26	
	You shall not bring an abomination into your house, and like it come under the ban; you shall utterly detest it and you shall utterly abhor it, for it is something banned.
Exodus 35:2	
	"For six days work may be done, but on the seventh day you shall have a holy day, a sabbath of complete rest to the Lord; whoever does any work on it shall be put to death.

Leviticus 11:10	But whatever is in the seas and in the rivers that does not have fins and scales among all the teeming life of the water, and among all the living creatures that are in the water, they are detestable things to you,
Proverbs 28:9	He who turns away his ear from listening to the law, Even his prayer is an abomination.
1 Corinthians 6:9	Or do you not know that the unrighteous will not inherit the kingdom of God? Do not be deceived; neither fornicators, nor idolaters, nor adulterers, nor effeminate, nor homosexuals,
Galatians 3:23-25	But before faith came, we were kept in custody under the law, being shut up to the faith which was later to be revealed. Therefore the Law has become our tutor to lead us to Christ, so that we may be justified by faith. But now that faith has come, we are no longer under a tutor.
Exodus 20:13	"You shall not murder.

Deuteronomy 18:12

For whoever does these things is detestable to the Lord; and because of these detestable things the Lord your God will drive them out before you.

Jeremiah 32:34

But they put their detestable things in the house which is called by My name, to defile it.

Proverbs 8:13

"The fear of the Lord is to hate evil;
Pride and arrogance and the evil way
And the perverted mouth, I hate.

Proverbs 6:17

Haughty eyes, a lying tongue,
And hands that shed innocent blood,

Ezekiel 8:6

> And He said to me, "Son of man, do you see what they are doing, the great abominations which the house of Israel are committing here, so that I would be far from My sanctuary? But yet you will see still greater abominations."

CHAPTER 5

The New Testament

a. The New Testament

The Bible has two main parts. The first part is called the Old Testament. The second part is the New Testament.

The New Testament contains 27 books.

It begins with Matthew and ends with Revelation. These books were written by eight men. These men wrote what God told them to write. The New Testament books were written in the Greek language. Later the New Testament books were translated into other languages. The New Testament is divided into 4 major sections. These sections are: **The Gospels, History, Epistles,** and **Prophecy**.

The Gospels

The first 4 books of the New Testament (**Matthew, Mark, Luke,** and **John**) are called the Gospels. The word "Gospel" means "good news." These books tell us the good news of the coming of Christ to save man from his sins. These books also tell us of the birth, life, teachings, death, burial, and resurrection of Christ. The authors of the Gospels are the same as the title of each book.

History

The book of history in the New Testament is **Acts** of the Apostles. It is often called the book of ACTS. This book was written by Luke.

It tells of the beginning of Christ's church in *Acts, chapter 2*.

Throughout the rest of the book, it tells how the church spread throughout the world. Acts tells many things that Peter and Paul did. The book of Acts also tells and shows us how people became Christians. Acts is often called the book of conversions. This is because it has so many examples of people being converted to Christ.

The following verses are examples of how people became Christians.

A. *Acts 2:36-38, 41, 42, 47* **People on day of Pentecost**
B. *Acts 8:1-13* **People of Samaria**
C. *Acts 8:26-39* **Ethiopian Eunuch**
D. *Acts 9:1-19; Acts 22:1-16* **Saul of Tarsus, who became the apostle Paul**
E. *Acts 10:1-48* **Cornelius**
F. *Acts 16:25-34* **Philippian jailer**

The Epistles

The word "epistle" means "letter." There are 21 epistles in the New Testament. The epistles of the New Testament can be divided into 2 groups: the Epistles of Paul and the General Epistles.

The apostle Paul wrote at least 13 of the 21 epistles. They are: Romans, 1 and 2 Corinthians, Galatians, Ephesians, Philippians, Colossians, 1 and 2 Thessalonians, 1 and 2 Timothy, Titus, and Philemon. Some believe Paul also wrote Hebrews. Some of Paul's epistles were written to individual persons and some to certain churches. Here is a brief summary of each one of the epistles:

Romans: Chapters 1-11 show that we are saved by faith. Chapter 12-16 are given to encourage the Romans to live the Christian life.

1 and 2 Corinthians: These books were written to the church at Corinth. Paul started this church. First Corinthians tells of the many problems the church had. Paul tells them to correct them. Second Corinthians shows that some of these problems had been overcome.

Galatians: This letter shows that Christians do not live under the law of Moses.

Ephesians, Philippians, and Colossians: These letters were written while Paul was in prison at Rome. The letters tell us that unity should be among Christians and that Christ is above and over all.

1 and 2 Thessalonians: These letters deal with the second coming of Christ. Some Christians had stopped working. They thought that Christ was to come again very soon. Paul told them this was not true.

1 and 2 Timothy and Titus: Timothy and Titus were two young preachers. They had been helping churches that Paul had established. He gave them much advice.

Philemon: Philemon was a Christian. He had a slave by the name of Onesimus. Onesimus ran away from Philemon. Paul met Onesimus and converted him. Paul then wrote a letter to Philemon asking him to take Onesimus back as a brother in Christ.

Hebrews: This epistle shows clearly the greatness of Christ's law over the law of Moses.

James; 1 and 2 Peter; 1, 2, and 3 John; Jude: These books are called the General Epistles. Each book is named after its author. Here is a brief summary of each book:

James: He was a brother of Christ. The book was written to Jews who had become Christians. One of its main teachings is that faith without works is dead.

1 Peter: This book was written to encourage those who were being persecuted (harmed). It shows that it is good to suffer for Christ.

2 Peter: Warning is given against false teachers. It also teaches concerning the second coming of Christ.

1, 2, and 3 John: First John is mostly about love. Second John is the shortest book in the Bible. It is written to "the elect lady." Third John is written to Gaius. John praises Gaius for his love for the Lord. Gaius is warned against Diotrephes.

Jude: False teachers had come into the church. Jude wrote in order to encourage Christians to fight for the faith once for all revealed to God's people. Jude teaches us that we must oppose error, even within the Lord's church.

b. The Two Covenants

The Bible is divided into two parts: (1) the Old Testament, and (2) the New Testament. The Old Testament contains the law of Moses. **It is also called the first covenant.** The New Testament contains the law of Christ. **It is also called the second covenant, or new covenant.**

The words "covenant" and "testament" have the same meaning. The two words will be used in this lesson, so remember that you can use one in the place of the other.

A "covenant" (testament) is an agreement or contract between two or more people.

Let us illustrate this by looking at a man who did not have a job. He went from place to place seeking employment.

Finally he found someone who would give him work. Before he started work, he was told that he would receive so much money each month. He was told to start work at 7 o'clock in the morning. He would then stop at 3:30 P.M.

He was to work these hours five days a week. Now if this man wants the job, he must agree to these rules. If the man takes the job, an agreement (contract) or "covenant" (testament) has been made between him and the employer.

The First Covenant

If man wants to be pleasing to God, he has to do what God tells him to do. God has had two great covenants with man. God's first great covenant was with the nation of Israel. God gave the covenant to Moses to give to the people.

These first commandments that God gave to Moses are known as the Ten Commandments (***Exodus 20:1-17***). God also gave Moses many other commands and ordinances (read ***Exodus 21-23***). The Israelites agreed to all of these commands and ordinances. "**...All that the Lord has said we will do, and be obedient**" (***Exodus 24:7***).

Moses then showed that the covenant had been made between God and the Israelites. "**And Moses took the blood, and sprinkled it on the people, and said, Behold the blood of the covenant, which the Lord hath made with you concerning all these words**" (***Exodus 24:8***).

This covenant is referred to as the first covenant. "**But now He has obtained a more excellent ministry, inasmuch as He is also Mediator of a better covenant, which was established on better promises. For if that first covenant had been faultless, then no place would have been sought for a second**" (***Hebrews 8:6-7***).

This "first covenant" is better known as the Law of Moses.

This covenant (Law of Moses) was given only to the Israelites (Jews). It was not given for all people. Neither was it to last forever.

Purpose Of The Law Of Moses

Man was sinful. He needed to know that he was a sinner. The Law of Moses showed man that he was a sinner. "**What shall we say then? Is the law sin? Certainly not! On the contrary, I would not have known sin except through the law...**" (*Romans 7:7*).

Another purpose of the law was to serve as a schoolmaster to bring the people unto Christ. "**Therefore the law was our tutor to bring us to Christ, that we might be justified by faith**" (*Galatians 3:24*).

The law of Moses taught the Israelites until Christ came. It was only to show man what was pleasing to God until Christ came. The law of Moses was to prepare the way for the coming of Christ. The law of Moses showed man what sin is. Since it did this, it has fulfilled its purpose.

The First Covenant Nailed To The Cross

The law of Moses had to be done away before the law of Christ (second covenant) could be established. "**He takes away the first that He may establish the second**" (*Hebrews 10:9*).

When the law of Moses was done away, the law of Christ came into effect. But when was the law of Moses done away? The writer of Colossians tells us, "...**having wiped out the handwriting of requirements that was against us, which was contrary to us. And He has taken it out of the way, having nailed it to the cross**" (*Colossians 2:14*). The "**handwriting of ordinances that was against us**" is the law of Moses. Jesus did away with the law of Moses when He died on the cross.

The New Covenant (Testament)

Jesus said, **"Do not think that I came to destroy the Law or the Prophets. I did not come to destroy but to fulfil"** (*Matthew 5:17*). Christ fulfilled the law and the prophets. When He fulfilled them, they were no longer needed.

After Jesus was raised from the dead, He said: **"...These are the words which I spoke to you while I was still with you, that all things must be fulfilled which were written in the Law of Moses and the Prophets and the Psalms concerning Me"** (*Luke 24:44*).

All of the things that had been written about Christ in the law, prophets, and psalms were fulfilled when He died on the cross. In the book of Acts we are told: **"Now when they had fulfilled all that was written concerning Him, they took Him down from the tree and laid Him in a tomb"** (*Acts 13:29*).

Christ fulfilled the law of Moses. When He fulfilled the law, He took it out of the way. It was no longer to be obeyed. Christ brought a new law. **"And for this reason He is the Mediator of the new covenant...."** (*Hebrews 9:15*).

The law of Christ is now to be obeyed. The New Testament calls the law of Christ the new covenant or the second covenant. **This new covenant, the law of Christ, is for ALL people. "There is neither Jew nor Greek, there is neither slave nor free, there is neither male nor female; for you are all one in Christ Jesus"** (*Galatians 3:28*).

Christians must live according to the teachings in this new covenant.

c. Jesus Christ, The Son of God, The Saviour

The greatest person who has ever lived is Jesus Christ. Jesus is the Son of God.

The entire Bible tells about Jesus. The Old Testament has many prophecies of His coming. The first four books of the New Testament (**Matthew, Mark, Luke,** and **John**) tell of His birth, ministry, death, and resurrection from the dead. The rest of the New Testament books tell about: -

(1) His church;

(2) His death for our sins;

(3) His second coming to judge the world.

Prophecies Of Jesus

Jesus died for the sins of mankind. God had planned this from the beginning.

Genesis 3:15 is the first prophecy of the death of Jesus for sins: "**And I** [God] **will put enmity Between you** [the serpent, called the devil] **and the woman, And between your seed and her Seed** [Jesus Christ]; **He** [Jesus] **shall bruise your** [the devil's] **head, And you** [the devil] **shall bruise His** [Jesus'] **heel** (*Genesis 3:15*).

Jesus is the seed of woman. He bruised the head of Satan when He died on the cross as a sacrifice for sins. There are hundreds of other prophecies about Jesus in the Old Testament. We can find these prophecies fulfilled in the New Testament.

The Birth Of Jesus

Jesus was born in Bethlehem. His mother, Mary, was a virgin. She had conceived Jesus in her womb before she married Joseph. She did not become pregnant by any man. She conceived Him by the Holy Spirit. Jesus had no human father, for He was the Son of God. This was according to what an angel had told Mary.

"And behold, you will conceive in your womb and bring forth a Son, and shall call His name Jesus. Then Mary said to the angel, "How can this be, since I do not know a man?" And the angel answered and said to her, "The Holy Spirit will come upon you, and the power of the Highest will overshadow you; therefore, also, that Holy One who is to be born will be called the Son of God" (Luke 1:31,34-35).

The Ministry Of Jesus

The Bible does not tell us much about the early years of Jesus' life. It tells us that **"Jesus increased in wisdom and stature, and in favour with God and men"** (*Luke 2:52*).

At the age of 30, Jesus was baptized by John the Baptist. After His baptism, Jesus went into the desert. At the end of forty days, Satan came and tempted Him. Jesus was the Son of God; He was also the son of Mary. Therefore, He was both human and divine. Since He was human, He was tempted in every way as we are.

"For we do not have a High Priest who cannot sympathize with our weaknesses, but was in all points tempted as we are, yet without sin" (*Hebrews 4:15*).

Then Jesus began preaching. **"The time is fulfilled, and the kingdom of God is at hand. Repent, and believe in the gospel"** (*Mark 1:15*).

Jesus preached the kingdom of God. He also worked many miracles. His miracles prove that God had sent Him. He healed the sick and cast out evil spirits (***Mark 1:34-35***), restored sight to the blind (***Mark 10:46-52***), fed the hungry (***Mark 6:34-44***), and raised the dead (***Luke 7:11-16; John 11***).

Some people do not know why He performed miracles. The miracles were to show that Jesus was the Son of God (***Acts 2:22***). Today, some people claim to have the power that Jesus had, but compare the following differences.

Jesus and the Early Church	Men Today
People cured immediately	Often takes days
Cures were visible to all	Often are of sicknesses none can see
Everyone was cured	Only some are cured
Faith rarely required	Always required
Complete cures	Partial cures

The truth is that men today do not have power like Jesus had; else they would do what he did!

His Parables

Jesus also taught in parables. Parables are stories taught to illustrate truth. They are well known stories of the earth to teach the truths of heaven. To see some of the parables Jesus taught, read ***Matthew 13*** *or* ***Luke 15***.

His Apostles

Another important work of Jesus was the selecting of the apostles. As Jesus knew He was soon to leave earth and go back to heaven, He picked out certain men to carry on His work. Later they received the Holy Spirit to help them do the work he had planned for them.

His Church

In **Matthew 16**, Jesus announced His plan to start the church (The word church as used in the Bible does not mean a building, but a group of people). Once established it was to abide forever (***Matthew 16:18; Daniel 2:44***). Some today do not think the church one is a member of is important, but the church Jesus started, and that is still on the earth, is of great importance. In fact, Jesus died for the church (***Acts 20:28***); and it is this church that He is going to save. (***Ephesians 5:23; Ephesians 1:22***).

The Death Of Jesus

Jesus preached for three years. Then He went to Jerusalem to attend the feast of the Passover. The religious leaders of Israel were jealous of Jesus. They wanted to kill Him. Jesus also knew that He must die as a sacrifice for the sins of the whole world. He knew that the time had now come for Him to die. He had tried to prepare His disciples for His death.

"From that time Jesus began to show to His disciples that He must go to Jerusalem, and suffer many things from the elders and chief priests and scribes, and be killed, and be raised the third day" (***Matthew 16:21***).

Jesus ate the Passover with His apostles. Then He went into the Garden of Gethsemane where He prayed. About midnight, the soldiers came to arrest Him. Jesus was taken before the high priest. Later, He was condemned by the Jewish Council. They sent Him to Pilate, the governor, for sentence. Pilate knew that Jesus was innocent.

He wanted to free Him, but feared he might displease the people. Therefore, he had Jesus beaten and crucified.

Crucifixion was a slow, painful death. Jesus' hands were nailed to the cross. He hung on the cross while people mocked and insulted Him. After about six hours, He died. Two of Jesus' disciples took His body down from the cross. On Friday evening, they buried the body of Jesus.

The Resurrection Of Jesus

Early on Sunday morning, the first day of the week, Jesus arose from the dead. The Apostle Paul wrote years later about the resurrection of Jesus.

"For I delivered to you first of all that which I also received: that Christ died for our sins according to the Scriptures, and that He was buried, and that He rose again the third day according to the Scriptures" (*1 Corinthians 15:3-4*).

Jesus has power even over death. He will one day raise from the dead those who believe in Him.

Jesus Christ died for you. He was raised for you. You can have eternal life by believing in Him. Have you accepted Christ as your Saviour by obeying the Gospel?

d. Faith

The importance of faith is stated for us in the book of Hebrews. **"But without faith it is impossible to please Him, for he who comes to God must believe that He is, and that He is a rewarder of those who diligently seek Him"** (*Hebrews 11:6*).

We are then told that **"faith is the substance of things hoped for, the evidence of things not seen"** (*Hebrews 11:1*). No man has ever seen heaven. Yet by faith we are sure that there is such a place, and we hope to go there when we die.

Many things that we do in life show some kind of faith. A person takes aspirin where he has a headache. Why? Because he believes the aspirin will get rid of the headache. When a person plants maize, he believes that it will grow. Children have faith in their parents. They believe their parents when their parents tell them something.

How To Have Faith

The book of Romans says, **"So then faith comes by hearing, and hearing by the word of God"** (*Romans 10:17*).

We have faith in something because we have heard about it. We cannot have faith without hearing. We plant maize to grow for food. Why do we plant it? How do we know that it will grow? Because we have heard that it will. An aspirin is taken to get rid of a headache. But why does a person take the aspirin? Because he has heard that it will get rid of the headache. We believe in God and Christ by hearing about them. We hear about them from the Bible.

We can hear about them from the Bible in two ways:

(1) by reading the Bible ourselves and

(2) by hearing someone tell about them from the Bible.

It is not possible to have faith in God and Christ without hearing about them. **"How then shall they call on Him in whom they have not believed? And how shall they believe in Him of whom they have not heard? And how shall they hear without a preacher?"** (*Romans 10:14*).

Different Kinds Of Faith

There are different degrees of faith. Jesus told His disciples once that they had "**little faith**" (*Matthew 8:26*). He told a Canaanite woman "**great is your faith**" (*Matthew 15:28*). Then there is faith that is necessary for salvation. "**Sirs, what must I do to be saved?**" So they said, "**Believe on the Lord Jesus Christ, and you will be saved, you and your household**" (*Acts 16:30-31*).

A person must believe in Jesus Christ in order to be saved. But belief by itself is not enough. "**You believe that there is one God. You do well. Even the demons believe and tremble!**" (*James 2:19*).

The demons [evil spirits] believe but are not saved. What then is needed in order for faith to save? The answer is trust and obedience. The demons believe in Christ but they do not trust and obey Him. <u>If we only believe</u> Christ, but <u>do not trust and obey</u> him, <u>we will not be saved</u>.

When Jesus gives a command we will obey it if we have the faith that saves. For example, Christ says: "**He who believes and is baptized will be saved; but he who does not believe will be condemned**" (*Mark 16:16*).

Christ gave two commands here.

<u>First</u>, a person must believe.
<u>Second</u>, he must be baptized in order to be saved.

If a person believes in Christ, but is not willing to be baptized, then he is not saved. He does not have an obedient faith. His faith is dead. Faith alone cannot save a person. "**You see then that a man is justified by works, and not by faith only**" (*James 2:24*).

A man is saved when he obeys the commands of Christ. Believing in the commands of Christ without obeying them will not save a person.

Faith is belief based on testimony. We believe it because we have been told about it. Faith is necessary in order to be pleasing to God. Without faith we cannot be saved. Yet faith by itself cannot save us. <u>We must have a faith that trusts and obeys Christ's commands in order to be saved</u>.

What kind of faith do you have? Is it faith that believes in Jesus Christ as the Son of God? Does your faith stop there? Have you put your trust in Christ? Have you done what He tells you to do to be saved? If not, why do you not trust and obey Him now? You will then have a faith that saves.

e. Repentance

"Truly, these times of ignorance God overlooked, but now commands all men everywhere to repent, because He has appointed a day on which He will judge the world in righteousness by the Man whom He has ordained. He has given assurance of this to all by raising Him from the dead" (*Acts 17:30-31*).

God has commanded all men to repent. On the Last Day everyone who has ever lived will appear before Christ in judgment. If we have failed to obey God's command to repent of our sins, we will be lost forever. Therefore, it is very important that we learn the meaning of repentance.

What Is Repentance?

"But what do you think? A man had two sons, and he came to the first and said, "Son, go, work today in my vineyard. "He answered

and said "I will not," but afterward he regretted it and went" (*Matthew 21:28-29*).

This parable teaches us the meaning of repentance. At first, the son in the parable refused to obey his father's command to work in the vineyard. Later, he **changed his mind** and went to work. All of us are like the son in the parable. We have disobeyed God's commands many times. But when we stop disobeying God and begin to do His will, we have repented.

Repentance is a change of mind. It is a **decision to stop doing wrong** and **to begin doing right.**

When a person repents, he changes his life completely. He decides that he will no longer rebel against God. He will obey the commands of God. One's repentance will be seen in the good works that he does. One who has truly repented will try to please God in everything.

What Causes Repentance?

"**For godly sorrow produces repentance leading to salvation, not to be regretted; but the sorrow of the world produces death**" (*2 Corinthians 7:10*).

Repentance is caused by godly sorrow. When a person realizes he has sinned by disobeying God, he becomes sorry for what he has done. This sorrow for his sin will lead the person to turn away from his sin. Thus, godly sorrow (being sorry for disobeying God) causes one to repent.

"**Or do you despise the riches of His goodness, forbearance, and longsuffering, not knowing that the goodness of God leads you to repentance?**" (*Romans 2:4*).

God is good to us. He has given us Jesus, His Son, to die for our sins. He has given us the Bible to tell about the way to eternal life. When we realize how good God is to us, we should be ashamed to disobey Him. Our sorrow for disobeying our Father will cause us to repent of our sins.

The Fruits Of Repentance

"Therefore bear fruits worthy of repentance, and do not begin to say to yourselves, "We have Abraham as our father." For I say to you that God is able to raise up children to Abraham from these stones" (*Luke 3:8*).

These words were spoken by John the Baptist. The people of Israel thought they were saved simply because Abraham, God's faithful servant, was their father. John told them that they must prove that they had repented. We prove that we have repented by doing good works. Before repenting, we do evil deeds. After repenting, we must do good deeds.

Suppose a man has a fruit tree in his garden. If the tree does not produce good fruit, he will cut it down and use it for firewood. But if the tree produces good fruit, he will save it. If we turn from our sins but do not do good works in their place, we will still be lost. But if we produce good works, God will love us and save us.

Have You Repented?

What about you? Have you repented of your sins? Are you producing the fruits of repentance? If not, you are lost forever! Christ will reject you on the last day.

"The Lord is not slack concerning His promise, as some count slackness, but is longsuffering toward us, not willing that any should perish but that all should come to repentance" (*2 Peter 3:9*).

Obey God's commands: "**Repent, and let every one of you be baptized in the name of Jesus Christ for the remission of sins; and you shall receive the gift of the Holy Spirit**" (*Acts 2:38*).

f. Confession

Confession Before Baptism

A person must confess that Jesus Christ is the Son of God before he can become a Christian. This confession is necessary to salvation.

"**That if you confess with your mouth the Lord Jesus and believe in your heart that God has raised Him from the dead, you will be saved. For with the heart one believes unto righteousness, and with the mouth confession is made unto salvation**" (*Romans 10:9-10*).

If a person will not confess that Jesus Christ is the Son of God, then he cannot become a Christian. In the book of Acts, we have an example of a man confessing Christ before being baptized.

"**Then Philip opened his mouth, and beginning at this Scripture, preached Jesus to him. Now as they went down the road, they came to some water. And the eunuch said, "See, here is water. What hinders me from being baptized?" Then Philip said, "If you believe with all your heart, you may." And he answered and said, "I believe that Jesus Christ is the Son of God**" (*Acts 8:35-37*).

After the eunuch made the confession, Philip baptized him. No one can become a Christian if he is not willing to confess that Jesus Christ is the Son of God.

Confession After Baptism

A person must confess that Jesus Christ is the Son of God before becoming a Christian. He must also confess Jesus Christ to others after he becomes a Christian. It is the duty of every Christian to tell others about the salvation that Jesus Christ offers to man. Jesus said that if we tell others about Him He will tell God about us. But if we don't tell others, He will deny us to God.

"Therefore whoever confesses Me before men, him I will also confess before My Father who is in heaven. But whoever denies Me before men, him I will also deny before My Father who is in heaven" (*Matthew 10:32-33*).

This confessing of Jesus Christ is to be done throughout the life of a Christian. Jesus Christ died so that all men might have the forgiveness of sins. The forgiveness of sins, however, depends upon men accepting and obeying Christ. But can men accept and obey Christ if they don't know about Him? **No!** Christians then must tell others about Christ so that they may accept and obey Him. Then they will receive the forgiveness of their sins. Nothing should prevent Christians from telling others about Christ. Christ has commanded Christians to confess Him, and so Christians **". . . ought to obey God rather than men"** (*Acts 5:29*).

We have learned that we are to confess Christ to others by word of mouth. We are also to confess Him in another way. We are to confess Christ by the way we live. Christ lived a perfect life. We are to follow His example.

"For to this you were called, because Christ also suffered for us, leaving us an example, that you should follow His steps" (*1 Peter 2:21*).

People are watching Christians all the time. If a Christian does wrong, others know it. They then speak evil of Christianity. But if Christians follow Christ, they will do that which is right. People will then see that Christianity is good. If a Christian tells others about Christ, but does not live right, then he speaks in vain. People will not listen to a Christian who tells them what to do but doesn't do it himself. A Christian must tell others about Christ and at the same time do what Christ tells him to do.

Confessing Our Sins

There are two ways we are to confess our sins. **First**, we are to confess our sins to one another. James says, "**Confess your trespasses one to another, and pray for one another, that you may be healed. The effective, fervent prayer of a righteous man avails much**" (*James 5:16*).

It is not easy for a person to say that he has sinned. Yet the Bible commands that we do it. Why are we to confess our sins to one another? It is so that we can pray about those sins. Christians should be interested in helping one another. If one Christian has sinned, all other Christians should want to help him overcome that sin. They can do that by praying for him.

The **second** way we are to confess our sins is to God.

"**If we confess our sins, He is faithful and just to forgive us our sins and to cleanse us from all unrighteousness**" (*1 John 1:9*). If we confess our sins to God, He will forgive our sins. What a great promise!

Therefore, a person must confess that Jesus Christ is the Son of God before he can become a Christian. After he becomes a Christian, he must confess Christ to others in two ways:

1. by word of mouth, and
2. by the kind of life that he lives.

After a person becomes a Christian, he will still commit sins. Christians are then to confess their sins to one another and to pray for one another so that they can overcome those sins. A Christian is also to confess to God his sins. God will then forgive him of his sins.

g. Baptism

- What is baptism?

- Who should be baptized?

- What is the purpose of baptism?

Only God can give us the answers to these questions. God's answers are found in the Bible. Let us learn what the Bible teaches about baptism.

Who Should Be Baptized?

The Bible gives us certain requirements which we first must obey before we can be baptized. One must believe in Jesus Christ before he can be baptized. Jesus said, **"He who believes and is baptized will be saved; but he who does not believe will be condemned"** (*Mark 16:16*).

How do we come to believe in Jesus? It is by hearing the Word of God. **"So then faith comes by hearing, and hearing by the word of God"** (***Romans 10:17***).

One must repent of his sins before he can be baptized. The Bible says: **"Repent, and let every one of you be baptized in the name of Jesus

Christ for the remission of sins..." (***Acts 2:38***). Repentance must come before baptism.

Before one can be baptized, he must confess his faith in Christ. "**. . . if you confess with your mouth the Lord Jesus and believe in your heart that God has raised Him from the dead, you will be saved. For with the heart one believes unto righteousness, and with the mouth confession is made unto salvation**" (***Romans 10:9-10***).

One must hear the Word of God, believe in the Lord Jesus Christ, repent of his sins, and confess his faith before he can be baptized into Christ.

A new born baby or small child cannot be baptized. A baby cannot understand about Jesus. A baby cannot repent of sins when he has not done anything, either good or bad. A baby cannot confess his faith in Jesus. Since a baby cannot hear, believe, repent, or confess, he cannot be baptized. In the Bible we learn that only people old enough to hear, believe, repent, and confess were ever baptized. "**But when they believed Philip as he preached the things concerning the kingdom of God and the name of Jesus Christ, both men and women were baptized**" (***Acts 8:12***).

How Should One Be Baptized?

There are two ways by which churches baptize people today. One is by pouring or sprinkling water on the person's head. The other is by burying or immersing a person in water. Which one is correct baptism? The Bible gives the answer.

In the Bible baptism is called a burial. "**We were buried with Him through baptism into death, that just as Christ was raised from the dead by the glory of the Father, even so we also should walk in newness of life**" (***Romans 6:4***).

If we want to bury a dead body, we will not sprinkle a little dirt on the head. We will cover the body completely. Baptism is a burial. Sprinkling water on the head of a person does not baptize him. He must be completely buried under the water.

"Now John also was baptizing in Aenon near Salim, because there was much water there. And they came and were baptized" (*John 3:23*).

John chose a place to baptize where there was much water. Sprinkling requires only a little water. But a burial in water requires much water. Therefore, John did not baptize by sprinkling. He baptized by burying in water.

"So, he commanded the chariot to stand still. And both Philip and the eunuch went down into the water, and he baptized him. And when they came up out of the water, the Spirit of the Lord caught Philip away, so that the eunuch saw him no more; and he went on his way rejoicing" (*Acts 8:38-39*).

When Philip baptized the eunuch, both of them went down into the water. After the baptism, both of them came up out of the water. To sprinkle a person, it is not necessary to go down into the water. To baptize a person by burying him in water, it is necessary to go down into it. Therefore, Philip baptized the eunuch by burial, not sprinkling.

What is the proper way to baptize? The Bible teaches it is by a burial in water. Therefore, sprinkling is not true baptism.

Why Be Baptized?

There are four reasons why we must be baptized:

First, we must be baptized if we want to be saved. Jesus Himself said: **"He who believes and is baptized will be saved; but he who does not believe will be condemned"** (*Mark 16:16*).

The apostle Peter said: "**There is also an antitype which now saves us—baptism (not the removal of the filth of the flesh, but the answer of a good conscience toward God), through the resurrection of Jesus Christ**" (*1 Peter 3:21*).

Second, we must be baptized if we want to have our sins forgiven. The Bible says: "**Repent, and let every one of you be baptized in the name of Jesus Christ for the remission of sins; and you shall receive the gift of the Holy Spirit**" (*Acts 2:38*).

Third, we must be baptized if we want to be in Christ. To be "**in Christ**" means "to be a Christian." The Bible says "**For as many of you as were baptized into Christ have put on Christ**" (*Galatians 3:27*).

Fourth, we must be baptized if we want to become a member of the body of Christ. The body of Christ is the church of Christ (*Ephesians 1:22-23*). The Bible says "**For by one Spirit we were all baptized into one body**" (*1 Corinthians 12:13*).

The early church had preaching in its worship. *Acts 20:7* shows that on one occasion Paul preached until very late in the night. There are many other verses that show the preaching as worship (*Acts 2:42; 2 Tim. 4:1-5*).

h. The Church, Part 1

There are thousands of different churches in the world. Each one of these denominations has its own teachings which are different from the teachings of other denominations. Each one of these churches is called by a different name. Yet, all of them claim to be following the Bible. Is this possible? No, it is not! The Bible contains only one teaching. Yet each one of these denominations has a different teaching.

- **What is the true church?**
- **How can we learn which is right?**
- There is only one way. Let us go to the Bible. The Bible will tell us what Christ's church is.

The Bible helps us to understand what Christ's church is like. It does this by "figures" or "pictures" of the church. Let us look at some of these pictures that we may understand what the true church is like.

The Kingdom

The Bible often pictures Christ's church as a kingdom. Sometimes it is called the *"kingdom of God"* because God is its Ruler. The members of the church are citizens of the kingdom. Sometimes the church is called the *"kingdom of heaven"* because it is a spiritual kingdom. It is not an earthly kingdom.

We know that the kingdom and the church are the same thing because Christ used them in this way. For example, let us hear Jesus' words to Peter: *"And I also say to you that you are Peter, and on this rock I will build My church, and the gates of Hades shall not prevail against it. And I will give you the keys of the kingdom of heaven, and whatever you bind on earth will be bound in heaven, and whatever you loose on earth will be loosed in heaven"* (Matthew 16:18-19).

God has set up His kingdom on the earth. It began on the Day of Pentecost after the resurrection of Christ (***Acts 2:1-47***). It began in city of Jerusalem. Since the church and the kingdom are the same, we know that Christ's church began in Jerusalem. It began on the first day of Pentecost after Jesus arose from the dead. Any church which began at any other place than Jerusalem **cannot** be the true church. Any church which began at any other time cannot be the true church.

Just before He returned to Heaven, Jesus said, *"Thus it is written, and thus it was necessary for the Christ to suffer and to rise from the dead the third day, and that repentance and remission of sins should be preached in His name to all nations, beginning at Jerusalem"* (*Luke 24:46-47*).

The Temple of God

The Bible sometimes pictures the church as the temple of God. *"Now, therefore, you are no longer strangers and foreigners, but fellow citizens with the saints and members of the household of God, having been built on the foundation of the apostles and prophets, Jesus Christ Himself being the chief cornerstone, in whom the whole building, being fitted together, grows into a holy temple in the Lord"* (*Ephesians 2:19-21*).

In the Old Testament, we can read how King Solomon built a temple for God (*1 Kings 8:12-13*). Today, the church is God's temple. God dwells in the church through His Spirit: *"Do you not know that you are the temple of God and that the Spirit of God dwells in you? If anyone defiles the temple of God, God will destroy him. For the temple of God is holy, which temple you are"* (*1 Corinthians 3:16-17*).

The Family of God

Sometimes the Bible pictures the church as God's household or family. *"But if I am delayed, I write so that you may know how you ought to conduct yourself in the house of God, which is the church of the living God, the pillar and ground of the truth"* (*1 Timothy 3:15*).

In His family, the church, God is the father. Members of the church are His children. One becomes a member of a family by being born into it. The same is true of God's family. One must be born again to become a member of it. *"...Most assuredly, I say to you, unless one is born of water and the Spirit, he cannot enter the kingdom of God"* (*John 3:5*).

A Holy Nation and A Royal Priesthood

Another picture of Christ's church is that of a holy nation and a royal priesthood. *"But you are a chosen generation, a royal priesthood, a holy nation, His own special people, that you may proclaim the praises of Him who called you out of darkness into His marvellous light"* (*1 Peter 2:9*).

In Old Testament times, God chose the nation of Israel to be His people. Today, Christ's church is the chosen nation of God. In the nation of Israel, there was a special class of people who served as priests. Only the priests were allowed to conduct the public worship of God. But in Christ's church, every member is a priest. Every member can pray to God for himself.

The Body of Christ

Many times, the Bible pictures Christ's church as His body. *"And He put all things under His feet, and gave Him to be head over all things to the church, which is His body, the fullness of Him who fills all in all"* (*Ephesians 1:22-23*).

The church is the body of Christ. Christ is the head of the body. He rules from heaven. Heaven is the headquarters of Christ's church. The human body has only **one** head. Christ's body, the church, has only **one** head. Christ is the Head of the church! Christ's church has no pope or president on the earth to rule over it.

The church is the body of Christ. Christ has only one body.

Therefore, Christ has only one church. *"There is one body and one Spirit, just as you were called in one hope of your calling"* (*Ephesians 4:4*). There are many thousands of different denominations in the world today. Christ's church is His body. Does Christ have thousands of different bodies? Of course not! A man has only **one** body. Christ has only **one** body—the church.

i. The Church, Part 2

There are thousands of different denominations in the world. But the Bible reveals only one church. Let us learn from the Bible about Christ's church. Let us become members of it. Then, we can know we are right. The Bible tells is what Christ's church is like. It tells us its names, organization, and worship.

The Names of The Church

The Bible gives several names for Christ's church and for its members. These names honour God and His Son, Jesus Christ.

In the New Testament, the church is often called "the church of God." *"Paul . . . to the church of God which is at Corinth"* (*1 Corinthians 1:1-2*). *"Therefore take heed to yourselves and to all the flock, among which the Holy Spirit has made you overseers, to shepherd the church of God which He purchased with His own blood"* (*Acts 20:28*).

When speaking of the various groups of Christians which make up the body of Christ, the term "churches of Christ" is used. *"...The churches of Christ greet you"* (*Romans 16:16*).

Members of the church in the Bible are often called "believers" because they trust in the Lord Jesus Christ. *"And believers were increasingly added to the Lord, multitudes of both men and women"* (*Acts 5:14*).

"Let no one despise your youth, but be an example to the believers in word, in conduct, in love, in spirit, in faith, in purity" (1 Timothy 4:12).

Sometimes members are called "saints," because they are set apart to do God's will. *"To the church of God which is at Corinth, to those who are sanctified in Christ Jesus, called to be saints, with all who in every place call on the name of Jesus Christ our Lord, both theirs and ours"* (1 Corinthians 1:2). *"...To all the saints in Christ Jesus who are in Philippi, with the bishops and deacons"* (Philippians 1:1).

They are often called "disciples" because they are learners of Christ. *"...So it was that for a whole year they assembled with the church and taught a great many people. And the disciples were first called Christians in Antioch"* (Acts 11:26). *"Now on the first day of the week, when the disciples came together to break bread, Paul, ready to depart the next day, spoke to them and continued his message until midnight"* (Acts 20:7).

Members are also called Christians. *"And the disciples were first called Christians at Antioch"* (Acts 11:26). *"Then Agrippa said to Paul, You almost persuade me to become a Christian"* (Acts 26:28). *"If you are reproached for the name of Christ, blessed are you, for the Spirit of glory and of God rests upon you. On their part He is blasphemed, but on your part He is glorified. But let none of you suffer as a murderer, a thief, an evildoer, or as a busybody in other people's matters. Yet if anyone suffers as a Christian, let him not be ashamed, but let him glorify God in this matter"* (1 Peter 4:14-16).

The Organization of The Church

God's plan for His church is very simple. Christ is the head of the whole church. *"And He put all things under His feet, and gave Him to be the head over all things to the church, which is His body, the fullness of Him who fills all in all"* (Ephesians 1:22-23).

<u>The New Testament is the only law which God gave to His church</u>. *"All Scripture is given by inspiration of God, and is profitable for doctrine, for reproof, for correction, for instruction in righteousness, that the man of God may be complete, thoroughly equipped for every good work"* (**2 Timothy 3:16-17**).

In each place where there are Christians, they meet together as a group and form the church of Christ in that place. Each of these groups is independent. Each has its own leaders. Each church of Christ is overseen by elders and served by deacons when it is fully organized.

Elders are called by different names in the New Testament. Sometimes they are called **"bishops,"** meaning "overseers." *"This is a faithful saying: If a man desires the position of a bishop, he desires a good work"* (**1 Timothy 3:1**). Sometimes they are called **"pastors,"** meaning "shepherds." *"And He Himself gave some to be apostles, some prophets, some evangelists, and some pastors and teachers, for the equipping of the saints for the work of ministry, for the edifying of the body of Christ"* (**Ephesians 4:11-12**). *"So when they had appointed elders in every church, and prayed with fasting, they commended them to the Lord in whom they had believed"* (**Acts 14:23**).

Deacons are leaders who serve under the elders. (**Philippians 1:1**.) The word "deacon" means "one who serves."

Not everyone can be an elder or a deacon. One must be a good man before he can do this work. The qualifications for elders are found in **1 Timothy 3:1-7** and **Titus 1:5-10**. The qualifications for deacons are stated in **1 Timothy 3:8-13**. No one can serve as an elder or deacon unless he meets God's qualifications. **No church can have elders or deacons until they have men who meet these qualifications.**

The Worship of The Church

The Bible tells us that Christ's church meets on Sunday, the first day of the week, for the worship of God. *"On the first day of the week, when the disciples came together to break bread, Paul, ready to depart the next day, spoke to them and continued his message until midnight" (Acts 20:7).* *"On the first day of the week let each one of you lay something aside, storing up as he may prosper, that there be no collections when I come" (1 Corinthians 16:2).*

This day is called "the Lord's Day." *"I was in the Spirit on the Lord's Day..." (Revelation 1:10).* The church may meet at any time for worship, but the first day of the week is especially *"the Lord's Day."*

On the Lord's Day, the church "breaks bread," or eats of the Lord's Supper. *"Now on the first day of the week, when the disciples came together to break bread" (Acts 20:7).*

The Lord's Supper was given by Jesus just before His death (*Matthew 26:26-29*). It is unleavened bread (made with no yeast) which represents His body, and the fruit of the vine (grape juice) which represents His blood. The purpose of the Lord's Supper is to remember Christ's death for our sins. *"The Lord Jesus on the same night in which He was betrayed took bread; and when He had given thanks, He broke it and said, Take, eat; this is My body which is broken for you; do this in remembrance of Me. In the same manner He also took the cup after supper, saying, This cup is the new covenant in My blood. This do, as often as you drink it, in remembrance of Me. For as often as you eat this bread and drink this cup, you proclaim the Lord's death till He comes" (1 Corinthians 11:23-26).*

<u>Christ's church worships Him by singing praises to Him</u>. *"Speaking to one another in psalms and hymns and spiritual songs, singing and making melody in your heart to the Lord"* (*Ephesians 5:19*). *"Let the word of Christ dwell in you richly in all wisdom, teaching and admonishing one another in psalms and hymns and spiritual songs, singing with grace in your hearts to the Lord"* (*Colossians 3:16*).

Each member of Christ's church worship Him from the heart. The purpose of worship is to praise God. It is not to entertain man. **God has not commanded the use of musical instruments in His worship.** Each Christian is to praise God. The melody is to be made with the Christian's heart, **not** with musical instruments.

<u>Christ's church worships Him by prayers of thanksgiving, praise, and request</u>. *"I exhort first of all that supplications, prayers, intercessions, and giving of thanks be made for all men, for kings and all who are in authority, that we may lead a quiet and peaceable life in all godliness and reverence"* (*1 Timothy 2:1-2*).

<u>Christ's church worships Him by studying and teaching God's Word</u>. *"Till I come, give attention to reading, to exhortation, to doctrine"* (*1 Timothy 4:13*).

<u>Christ's church takes a contribution on the first day of the week</u>. In this way money is raised for the work of the Lord. *"On the first day of the week let each one of you lay something aside, storing up as he may prosper, that there be no collections when I come"* (*1 Corinthians 16:2*).

The Bible reveals no other method for raising money for the Lord's work.

j. The Genealogy from Adam to Jesus Christ

This is the Biblical Genealogy of Jesus Christ.

		ADAM (1) "The Son of God" and The First Adam	
		SETH (2)	
		ENOS (3)	
		CAINAN (4)	
		MAHALEEL (5)	
		JARED (6)	
		ENOCH (7)	
		METHUSALEH (8)	
		LAMECH (9)	
		NOAH (10)	
		SHEM (11)	
		ARPHAXAD (12)	
		CAINAN (13)	
		SALA (14)	
		EBER (15)	
		PELEG (16)	
		RAGAU (17)	
		SARUCH (18)	
		NAHOR (19)	
		TERAH (20)	
		(1) ABRAHAM (21)	
		(2) ISAAC (22)	
		(3) JACOB (23)	

		(4) JUDA (24) m. Tamar		---> Zera (Matthew 1:3)
		(5) PHAREZ (25)		
		(6) ESROM (26)		
		(7) ARAM (27)		
		(8) AMMINADAB (28)		
		(9) NAASON (29)		
		(10) SALMON (30) m. Rachab		(Sala: Luke 3:32)
		(11) BOAZ (31) m. Ruth		
		(12) OBED (32)		
		(13) JESSE (33)		
		(14) DAVID (34) m. Bathsheba (Luke 3:31)		
(1) SOLOMON Matthew 1:6			NATHAN (35) (2 Sam.5.14)	
(2) REHOBOAM				
(3) ABIA			MATTATHA (36)	
(4) ASA				MENAN (37)
(5) JOSOPHAT	OMRI			MELEA (38)
	|			ELIAKIM (39)
	AHAB m. Jezebel |			JONAN (40)
(6) JORAM	m. Athaliah			JOSEPH (41)

	(Ahaziah)				JUDAH (42)
	(Joash)				SIMEON (43)
	(Amaziah)				LEVI (44)
(7) OZIAS					MATTHAT (45)
(8) JOATHAM					JORIM (46)
(9) ACHAZ					ELIEZER (47)
(10) EZEKIAS					JOSE (48)
(11) MANASSES					ER (49)
(12) AMON					ELMODAM (50)
(13) JOSIAS					COSAM (51)
(14) JEHOIKIM (who had brothers, Matthew 1:11)					ADDI (52)
				MELCHI (53)	
(1) JECHONIAS (55) m. --->	(2) SALATHIEL (56)		Widowed daughter husband deceased		NERI (54) <------
(Evidently Salathiel died childless and Pedaiah, his brother, married his widow according to Deut. 25:5-6)			wife m. PEDAIAH (Quite legally according to the Mosaic law, Pedaiah's name does not appear as the father of Zerubbabel in either Matthew or Luke.)		
(3) ZERUBBABEL (57) (1 Chr. 3:19)					
daughter SHELOMITH --> m RHESA (58)					
(4) ABIUD			JOANNA (59)		
(5) ELIAKIM			JUDA (60)		
			JOSEPH (61)		

(6) AZOR		MATTATHIAS (63)	SEMEI (62)
(7) SADOC			MAATH (64)
(8) ACHIM			NAGGE (65)
			ESLI (66)
(9) ELIUD			NAHUM (67)
			AMOS (68)
(10) ELEAZER			MATTATHIAS (69)
			JOSEPH (70)
			JANNA (71)
(11) MATTHAN			MELCHI (72)
			LEVI (73)
			MATTHAT (74)
(12) JACOB			HELI (75)
	(13) JOSEPH	m.	MARY (76)
(14) JESUS (77) **The Son of God and the Last Adam**			

The Line of Jesus through Joseph

The book of the genealogy of Jesus Christ, the son of David, the son of Abraham. Abraham was the father of Isaac, and Isaac the father of Jacob, and Jacob the father of Judah and his brothers, and Judah the father of Perez and Zerah by Tamar, and Perez the father of Hezron, and Hezron the father of Ram, and Ram the father of Amminadab, and Amminadab the father of Nahshon, and Nahshon the father of Salmon, and Salmon the father of Boaz by Rahab, and Boaz the father of Obed by Ruth, and Obed the father of Jesse, and Jesse the father of David the king. And David was the father of Solomon by the wife of Uriah, and Solomon the father of Rehoboam, and Rehoboam the father of Abijah, and Abijah the father of Asa, and Asa the father of Jehoshaphat, and Jehoshaphat the father of Joram, and Joram the father of Uzziah, and Uzziah the father of Jotham, and Jotham the father of Ahaz, and Ahaz the father of Hezekiah, and Hezekiah the father of Manasseh, and Manasseh the father of Amos, and Amos the father of Josiah, and Josiah the father of Jechoniah and his brothers, at the time of the deportation to Babylon. And after the deportation to Babylon: Jechoniah was the father of Shealtiel, and Shealtiel the father of Zerubbabel, and Zerubbabel the father of Abiud, and Abiud the father of Eliakim, and Eliakim the father of Azor, and Azor the father of Zadok, and Zadok the father of Achim, and Achim the father of Eliud, and Eliud the father of Eleazar, and Eleazar the father of Matthan, and Matthan the father of Jacob, and Jacob the father of Joseph the husband of Mary, of whom Jesus was born, who is called Christ. So all the generations from Abraham to David were fourteen generations, and from David to the deportation to Babylon fourteen generations, and from the deportation to Babylon to the Christ fourteen generations. (Matthew 1:1-17)

The Line of Jesus Through Mary

Jesus, when he began his ministry, was about thirty years of age, being the son (as was supposed) of Joseph, the son of Heli, the son of Matthat, the son of Levi, the son of Melchi, the son of Jannai, the son of Joseph, the son of Mattathias, the son of Amos, the son of Nahum, the son of Esli, the son of Naggai, the son of Maath, the son of Mattathias, the son of Semein, the son of Josech, the son of Joda, the son of Joanan, the son of Rhesa, the son of Zerubbabel, the son of Shealtiel, the son of Neri, the son of Melchi, the son of Addi, the son of Cosam, the son of Elmadam, the son of Er, the son of Joshua, the son of Eliezer, the son of Jorim, the son of Matthat, the son of Levi, the son of Simeon, the son of Judah, the son of Joseph, the son of Jonam, the son of Eliakim, the son of Melea, the son of Menna, the son of Mattatha, the son of Nathan, the son of David, the son of Jesse, the son of Obed, the son of Boaz, the son of Sala, the son of Nahshon, the son of Amminadab, the son of Admin, the son of Arni, the son of Hezron, the son of Perez, the son of Judah, the son of Jacob, the son of Isaac, the son of Abraham, the son of Terah, the son of Nahor, the son of Serug, the son of Reu, the son of Peleg, the son of Eber, the son of Shelah, the son of Cainan, the son of Arphaxad, the son of Shem, the son of Noah, the son of Lamech, the son of Methuselah, the son of Enoch, the son of Jared, the son of Mahalaleel, the son of Cainan, the son of Enos, the son of Seth, the son of Adam, the son of God. (Luke 3:23-38).

CHAPTER 6

FINAL The End Times/Prophecy

FINAL THE END TIMES/ PROPHECY

The last book of the Bible is Revelation. It is a book of prophecy. No other book of the Bible has been as misunderstood and misapplied as the book of Revelation. False teachers have wrested passages from it in efforts to support their errors. Because it has been so widely misused, many Christians are afraid to study Revelation. Some Christians even believe it is not possible to understand it.

God gave us the book of Revelation. It is a part of His will to mankind. Therefore, it is important that we study it and do our best to understand it. The word "revelation" is a translation of a Greek word which means "an unveiling, an uncovering, or a revealing." The very name of the book indicates we can understand it. The Holy Spirit pronounces a blessing upon those who read and hear the message of Revelation: ***"Blessed is he who reads, and those who hear the words of this prophecy, and keep those things which are written in it; for the time is near"*** **(*Revelation 1:3*)**.

The key to understanding Revelation is in the first verse: ***"The Revelation of Jesus Christ, which God gave Him to show His servants - things which must shortly take place. And He sent and signified it by His angel to His servant John."*** Two things are mentioned in this verse which will help us understand the book.

- **First**, it deals with things which must shortly take place. John was writing to churches in the first century. They were being persecuted because of their faith in Christ. The things revealed in Revelation were meant to encourage them. They did not pertain to things which would happen hundreds of years later. They pertained to things which would happen shortly.

- **Second**, Jesus sent and signified it by His angel to His servant John. To signify means "to give in signs or symbols." Revelation was given in figurative language. If we take Revelation literally, we will misunderstand it.

Revelation shows the completion of God's plan of redemption. In the first book of the Bible, we read of man's fall into sin. Because of sin, man was no longer allowed to eat of the tree of life in the Garden of Eden (***Genesis 3***). In Revelation, we learn the tree of life is now in Paradise. Whoever overcomes the temptations of this world will be given the privilege of eating of the tree of life (***Revelation 2:7***).

The first book of the Bible has been called "Paradise Lost." The last book of the Bible has been called "Paradise Regained."

Who Wrote Revelation?

The message of Revelation was given to us by Jesus Christ. It came from God to His servants. It was sent by His angel to John who wrote it in a book (***Revelation 1:1***). Again and again, the angel told John to write down the things which were revealed to him (***Revelation 2:1; 2:8; 2:12; 2:18; 3:1; 3:7; 3:14; 14:13; 19:9***).

The human writer of Revelation was the apostle John. John also wrote the Gospel of John and the books of First, Second and Third John. He was the brother of James and one of the original twelve apostles (***Matthew 10:1-4***). According to early Christian writers, John was the only apostle who died a natural death. He lived to be very old. After the destruction of Jerusalem in A.D. 70, John lived in Ephesus. During a time of persecution, John was arrested and taken to Patmos, a small island in the Mediterranean Sea seventy miles from Ephesus. It was here that the vision of Revelation was given to him (***Revelation 1:9-11***).

When Was Revelation Written?

Some Bible students believe Revelation was written before Jerusalem was destroyed in A.D. 70. They place the date of writing between A.D. 64 and A.D. 69. They argue that John was commanded to measure the temple (***Revelation 11:1***). Therefore, the temple had not yet been destroyed. However, they forget that Revelation is written in figurative language. Thus, the temple is not to be understood in a literal sense. It likely refers to the church. Those who hold the early date also believe the Roman emperor behind the persecution in Revelation is Nero. Nero ruled from A.D. 54 to A.D. 68. He blamed Christians for burning the city of Rome in 64. He had many Christians cruelly tortured and killed. However, Nero's persecution did not extend to the Roman provinces. The persecution in Revelation affected the churches in places beyond Rome such as in Asia.

Most Bible students believe that Revelation was written during the time of the emperor Domitian who ruled from A. D. 81 to A.D. 96. The evidence for this date is very strong. An early Christian writer, Irenaeus, was a disciple of Polycarp. Polycarp had been a student of the apostle John. Irenaeus wrote of Revelation: "For that was seen not very long since, but almost in our day, toward the end of Domitian's reign." This would place the date of Revelation about A.D. 95.

Domitian was the first Roman emperor to begin a persecution of the church throughout the whole Roman Empire. He required everyone to offer sacrifices to his image to show they were loyal to him and to the empire. Christians could not do this for it would be idolatry (***Galatians 5:19-21***). Therefore, Christians were persecuted. Many had their property taken from them. Thousands were killed.

Revelation indicates a time when the churches had lost their early zeal. Ephesus had *"left its first love"* (***Revelation 2:4***). Sardis was "dead" (***Revelation 3:1-2***). Laodicea, which had been destroyed by an earthquake in Nero's reign, had been rebuilt. The church had become *"lukewarm"* (***Revelation 3:14-16***). All of these things point to a later date as the time of writing. The time when Revelation was written is very important for understanding the book.

Revelation was addressed to *"the seven churches of Asia"* (***Revelation 1:4; Revelation 2 & 3***). These churches had been established as a result of the work of the apostle Paul (***Acts 19 & 20***). Since seven is a number which stands for perfection or completeness, it is likely these seven churches were meant to represent all churches everywhere.

The Message of Revelation

Christians were facing severe persecution and needed encouragement. Revelation provided this. It shows that even though things look bad on earth, God is still in control. Christians may suffer for a time, but they will overcome. Satan and his allies on earth cannot prevail against the Lord. Christians are *"more than conquerors through Him who loved us"* (***Romans 8:37***).

a. The Second Coming of Christ

Jesus is coming again! This is clearly taught in the New Testament. **"In My Father's house are many mansions; if it were not so, I would have told you. I go to prepare a place for you. And if I go** and prepare a place for you, I will come again and receive you to Myself; that where I am, there you may be also" (*John 14:2-3*).

When Is Christ Coming Again?

When is Christ coming again? Since the time that Jesus went to Heaven, men have tried to say when He will return. Yet the Bible clearly teaches that no man knows when Christ will return. "**But of that day and hour no one knows, not even the angels of heaven, but My Father only**" (*Matthew 24:36*).

When will Jesus come again? The angels in heaven do not know. Jesus did not even know. <u>No man knows. Only God knows</u>. We must not say when Jesus will return because we do not know. <u>We only know that He will return. We must believe this</u>! "**For you yourselves know perfectly that the day of the Lord so comes as a thief in the night**" (*1 Thessalonians 5:2*).

The "**day of the Lord**" refers to the second coming of Christ. Christ's second coming will be like a thief in the night. When does a thief steal? When you expect him to steal? No! A thief steals when he is not expected. So it will be with the second coming of Christ. Christ will come again when He is not expected.

How Is Christ Coming?

The apostles were told by the angels that Jesus would return the same way He went into Heaven. "**Men of Galilee, why do you stand gazing up into heaven? This same Jesus, who was taken up from you into heaven, will so come in like manner as you saw Him go into heaven**" (*Acts 1:11*).

It was Jesus who went into Heaven. It is Jesus who will be coming from Heaven.

Some people teach that Jesus has already returned. They teach that He returned in 1914, but many did not see Him. This teaching is **not** what the Bible says. The Bible says, "**Behold, He is coming with clouds, and every eye will see Him, even they who pierced Him. And all the tribes of the earth will mourn because of Him. Even so, Amen**" (*Revelation 1:7*). Has Jesus returned yet? Have you seen Him? **No!** When Jesus comes again, everyone will see Him. Those in the cities will see Him. Those in the villages will see Him. No one will miss seeing Him!

Again, we are told that when Christ returns He will be heard by everyone. "**For the Lord Himself will descend from heaven with a shout, with a voice of an archangel, and with the trumpet of God. And the dead in Christ will rise first**" (*1 Thessalonians 4:16*).

Just as everyone will see Christ, everyone will hear Him too. The "**shout,**" "**the archangel's call,**" and the sound of "**the trumpet of God**" all show the authority Christ has. They also show He has an important announcement to make.

Why Is Christ Coming Again?

The Bible gives several reasons why Christ is coming again. He is coming to raise the dead. Some people teach that the bad will never rise from the grave. Others teach that the good and bad will be raised at different times. But the Bible says, "**The hour is coming in which all who are in the graves will hear His voice and come forth - those who have done good, to the resurrection of life, and those who have done evil, to the resurrection of condemnation**" (*John 5:28-29*).

<u>All faithful, obedient Christians will meet Christ in the air. From there they will go to Heaven with Him</u>. "**For the Lord Himself will descend from heaven with a shout, with the voice of an archangel, and with the trumpet of God. And the dead in Christ will rise first.**

Then we who are alive and remain shall be caught up together with them in the clouds to meet the Lord in the air. And thus we shall always be with the Lord" (*1 Thessalonians 4:16-17*).

When Christ comes again, He will deliver up the kingdom to God. He is **not** coming to set up the kingdom. The kingdom is already here. The kingdom is the church. "**Then comes the end, when He delivers the kingdom to God the Father, when He puts an end to all rule and all authority and power**" (*1 Corinthians 15:24*).

The world will be destroyed at the second coming of Christ. "**But the day of the Lord will come as a thief in the night, in which the heavens will pass away with a great noise, and the elements will melt with fervent hear; both the earth and the works that are in it will be burned up**" (*2 Peter 3:10*).

When Christ comes again, people will no longer live on the earth. The earth will be burned up by fire.

The day of judgment is coming! God will judge the world. He has appointed His Son, Jesus Christ, to be the judge. "**God . . . commands all men everywhere to repent . . . He has appointed a day on which He will judge the world in righteousness by the Man whom He has ordained**" (*Acts 17:30-31*). The judgment will take place on the day that Christ comes again.

b. Daniel and King Nebuchadnezzar Dream

Israel had been conquered by the Assyrian Empire in 710 BC, and Judea was captured by the Babylonians in 605 BC. The Medo-Persian empire then conquered the Babylonians in 539-310 BC.

The book of Daniel was during the time of King Nebuchadnezzar, the Babylonian empire, 605-539 BC. God had given Daniel, Hananiah,

Mishael and Azariah knowledge and skill in all literature and wisdom: and Danial had understanding in all visions and dreams (***Daniel 1:17***).

King Nebuchadnezzar interviewed and found none like Daniel, Hananiah, Mishael and Azariah, therefore they served before the king. And in all matters of wisdom and understanding about which the king had examined them, he found them ten times better than all the magicians and astrologers who were in all his realm. Thus Daniel continued until the first year of King Cyrus, "Medo-Persian Empire" (***Daniel 1:19-21***).

Old Testament – King Nebuchadnezzar Dream

Daniel (Chapter 2) describes a dream of Nebuchadnezzar, the king of the Babylonian empire, which Daniel the prophet interpreted. Nebuchadnezzar had seen an enormous statue.

It had a head of gold, arms of silver, belly and thighs of bronze, and legs of iron — with feet of iron and clay (***Daniel 2:31-33***). A "cut out" rock struck the statue on its feet and caused it to fall down and break into pieces. The wind swept away the debris, and the rock that struck the statue "became a huge mountain and filled the whole earth" (***Daniel 2:34-35***).

The interpretation of the statue:

Statue	Represent	Meaning/ Empire
Gold,	Head	Assyrian Empire, 858-612 BC
Silver	Arms	Babylonian Empire, 605-539 BC

Bronze	**Belly and Thighs**	Medo-Persian Empire, 539-330 BC
		Greek Empire, 330-190 BC
Iron and Clay	**Legs and Feet**	This represents:
		1. Roman Empire -
		1.a. Roman Empire, 190 BC to 590 A.D. (Eastern Roman Empire to 1450 AD).
		2. Roman Catholic Church, 490 A.D. to Present Time
		and to come.........
		3. One World Government/ Order (Global Empire)

Biblical prophecy is very fascinating, as it is always correct. This is because it comes straight from God, given to prophets in sharing His message.

God's message may not fit to what we expect but we must remember that God does not fit to our expectations, so we must always pay attention, being patient; watching, listening and waiting for God's plans to show themselves.

God punished Israel during King Solomons reign for going against Gods laws and commandments, marrying many foreign women, worshipping false gods and for turning the hearts of the nation away from God.

Therefore, God removed all tribes away from Solomon, leaving just one tribe to his son, for the sake of King David, and Jerusalem (*1 Kings 11:1-43*).

However, Solomon's son King Rehoboam and his descendants again turned the country Judah away from God. Likewise, Jeroboam was made King of Israel, after returning from Egypt (from his enemy King Solomon). Over time, King Jeroboam's descendants also turned away from God's laws and commandments.

This led to Israel carried captive to Assyria (*2 Kings 17:5-23*), whilst Judah was later captured and taken to Babylon (*Jeremiah 39*).

2 Kings 17:5-23
Israel Carried Captive to Assyria

5 Now the king of Assyria went throughout all the land, and went up to Samaria and besieged it for three years.

6 In the ninth year of Hoshea, the king of Assyria took Samaria and carried Israel away to Assyria, and placed them in Halah and by the Habor, the River of Gozan, and in the cities of the Medes.

7 For so it was that the children of Israel had sinned against the Lord their God, who had brought them up out of the land of Egypt, from under the hand of Pharaoh king of Egypt; and they had feared other gods,

8 and had walked in the statutes of the nations whom the Lord had cast out from before the children of Israel, and of the kings of Israel, which they had made.

9 Also the children of Israel secretly did against the Lord their God things that *were* not right, and they built for themselves high places in all their cities, from watchtower to fortified city.

10 They set up for themselves *sacred* pillars and wooden images on every high hill and under every green tree.

11 There they burned incense on all the high places, like the nations whom the Lord had carried away before them; and they did wicked things to provoke the Lord to anger,

12 for they served idols, of which the Lord had said to them, "You shall not do this thing."

13 Yet the Lord testified against Israel and against Judah, by all of His prophets, every seer, saying, "Turn from your evil ways, and keep My commandments *and* My statutes, according to all the law which I commanded your fathers, and which I sent to you by My servants the prophets."

14 Nevertheless they would not hear, but stiffened their necks, like the necks of their fathers, who did not believe in the Lord their God.

15 And they rejected His statutes and His covenant that He had made with their fathers, and His testimonies which He had testified against them; they followed idols, became idolaters, and *went* after the nations who *were* all around them, *concerning* whom the Lord had charged them that they should not do like them.

16 So they left all the commandments of the Lord their God, made for themselves a molded image *and* two calves, made a wooden image and worshiped all the host of heaven, and served Baal.

17 And they caused their sons and daughters to pass through the fire, practiced witchcraft and soothsaying, and sold themselves to do evil in the sight of the Lord, to provoke Him to anger.

18 Therefore the Lord was very angry with Israel, and removed them from His sight; there was none left but the tribe of Judah alone.

19 Also Judah did not keep the commandments of the Lord their God, but walked in the statutes of Israel which they made.

20 And the Lord rejected all the descendants of Israel, afflicted them, and delivered them into the hand of plunderers, until He had cast them from His sight.

21 For He tore Israel from the house of David, and they made Jeroboam the son of Nebat king. Then Jeroboam drove Israel from following the Lord, and made them commit a great sin.

22 For the children of Israel walked in all the sins of Jeroboam which he did; they did not depart from them,

23 until the Lord removed Israel out of His sight, as He had said by all His servants the prophets. So Israel was carried away from their own land to Assyria, *as it is* to this day.

Jeremiah 39
The Fall of Jerusalem

1 In the ninth year of Zedekiah king of Judah, in the tenth month, Nebuchadnezzar king of Babylon and all his army came against Jerusalem, and besieged it.

2 In the eleventh year of Zedekiah, in the fourth month, on the ninth *day* of the month, the city was penetrated.

3 Then all the princes of the king of Babylon came in and sat in the Middle Gate: Nergal-Sharezer, Samgar-Nebo, Sarsechim, Rabsaris, Nergal-Sarezer, Rabmag, with the rest of the princes of the king of Babylon.

4 So it was, when Zedekiah the king of Judah and all the men of war saw them, that they fled and went out of the city by night, by way of the king's garden, by the gate between the two walls. And he went out by way of the plain.

5 But the Chaldean army pursued them and overtook Zedekiah in the plains of Jericho. And when they had captured him, they brought him up to Nebuchadnezzar king of Babylon, to Riblah in the land of Hamath, where he pronounced judgment on him.

6 Then the king of Babylon killed the sons of Zedekiah before his eyes in Riblah; the king of Babylon also killed all the nobles of Judah.

7 Moreover he put out Zedekiah's eyes, and bound him with bronze fetters to carry him off to Babylon.

8 And the Chaldeans burned the king's house and the houses of the people with fire, and broke down the walls of Jerusalem.

9 Then Nebuzaradan the captain of the guard carried away captive to Babylon the remnant of the people who remained in the city and those who defected to him, with the rest of the people who remained.

10 But Nebuzaradan the captain of the guard left in the land of Judah the poor people, who had nothing, and gave them vineyards and fields [f]at the same time.

Jeremiah Goes Free

11 Now Nebuchadnezzar king of Babylon gave charge concerning Jeremiah to Nebuzaradan the captain of the guard, saying,

12 "Take him and look after him, and do him no harm; but do to him just as he says to you."

13 So Nebuzaradan the captain of the guard sent Nebushasban, Rabsaris, Nergal-Sharezer, Rabmag, and all the king of Babylon's chief officers;

14 then they sent *someone* to take Jeremiah from the court of the prison, and committed him to Gedaliah the son of Ahikam, the son of Shaphan, that he should take him home. So he dwelt among the people.

15 Meanwhile the word of the Lord had come to Jeremiah while he was shut up in the court of the prison, saying,

16 "Go and speak to Ebed-Melech the Ethiopian, saying, 'Thus says the Lord of hosts, the God of Israel: "Behold, I will bring My words upon this city for adversity and not for good, and they shall be *performed* in that day before you.

17 But I will deliver you in that day," says the Lord, "and you shall not be given into the hand of the men of whom you *are* afraid.

18 For I will surely deliver you, and you shall not fall by the sword; but your life shall be as a prize to you, because you have put your trust in Me," says the Lord.' "

c. The Medo-Persian Empire

The Medo-Persian Empire had invaded the Babylonian Empire in 539 BC, and lasted 180 years, until 330 BC. This new Empire was very great, dominating 129 provinces from India (Hindush), Persia, Media, Assyria, Syria, Judea, Egypt, Lydia and Thrace.

"Thus saith Cyrus king of **Persia**, All the kingdoms of the earth hath the LORD God of heaven given me; and he hath charged me to build him a house in Jerusalem, which [is] in Judah. Who [is there] among you of all his people? The LORD his God [be] with him, and let him go up". (*2 Chronicles 36:23*)

After the Medo-Persian Empire, the Greek Empire under Alexandra the Great, invaded the lands in 330 BC until 180 BC. The book of Daniel (Daniel 8:21-24), details this quite vividly:

Daniel 8:21-24

21 And the male goat *is* the kingdom of Greece. The large horn that *is* between its eyes *is* the first king.

22 As for the broken *horn* and the four that stood up in its place, four kingdoms shall arise out of that nation, but not with its power.

23 "And in the latter time of their kingdom,
When the transgressors have reached their fullness,
A king shall arise,
Having fierce features,
Who understands sinister schemes.

24 His power shall be mighty, but not by his own power;
He shall destroy fearfully,
And shall prosper and thrive;
He shall destroy the mighty, and *also* the holy people.

Therefore, by looking at the above scripture, we can identify:

1. Male goat = Greece
2. Its Large Horn represents = Assyria
3. The Broken Horn = Babylon
4. Four Horns/ Four Kingdoms = Medo-Persian
   = Greece
   = Roman

= One World Government/ Order (Anti-Christ, Future last empire)

In Daniel 7, it is Daniel who has a dream. He sees four beasts coming up out of the sea that look similar to the following animals (with certain strange additions): a lion, a bear and a leopard. The fourth beast was terrifying and didn't look like any natural animal. This beast had ten horns and large iron teeth (***Daniel 7:4-7***).

Daniel then saw a vision of the Son of Man, to whom was given "authority, glory and sovereign power" and "all peoples, nations and men of every language worshipped him" (***Daniel 7:13-14***). His dominion was to be everlasting, and his kingdom would never be destroyed.

d. Daniel and Revelation –The Four Beasts

Daniel 7:1–28
Vision of the Four Beasts

7:1 In the first year of Belshazzar king of Babylon, Daniel had a dream and visions of his head *while* on his bed. Then he wrote down the dream, telling the main facts.

2 Daniel spoke, saying, "I saw in my vision by night, and behold, the four winds of heaven were stirring up the Great Sea.

3 And four great beasts came up from the sea, each different from the other.

4 The first *was* like a lion, and had eagle's wings. I watched till its wings were plucked off; and it was lifted up from the earth and made to stand on two feet like a man, and a man's heart was given to it.

5 "And suddenly another beast, a second, like a bear. It was raised up on one side, and *had* three ribs in its mouth between its teeth. And they said thus to it: 'Arise, devour much flesh!'

6 "After this I looked, and there was another, like a leopard, which had on its back four wings of a bird. The beast also had four heads, and dominion was given to it.

7 "After this I saw in the night visions, and behold, a fourth beast, dreadful and terrible, exceedingly strong. It had huge iron teeth; it was devouring, breaking in pieces, and trampling the residue with its feet. It *was* different from all the beasts that *were* before it, and it had ten horns.

8 I was considering the horns, and there was another horn, a little one, coming up among them, before whom three of the first horns were plucked out by the roots. And there, in this horn, *were* eyes like the eyes of a man, and a mouth speaking pompous words.

Vision of the Ancient of Days
9 "I watched till thrones were put in place,
And the Ancient of Days was seated;
His garment *was* white as snow,
And the hair of His head *was* like pure wool.
His throne *was* a fiery flame,
Its wheels a burning fire;

10 A fiery stream issued
And came forth from before Him.
A thousand thousands ministered to Him;
Ten thousand times ten thousand stood before Him.
The court was seated,
And the books were opened.

11 "I watched then because of the sound of the pompous words which the horn was speaking; I watched till the beast was slain, and its body destroyed and given to the burning flame.

12 As for the rest of the beasts, they had their dominion taken away, yet their lives were prolonged for a season and a time.

13 "I was watching in the night visions,
And behold, *One* like the Son of Man,
Coming with the clouds of heaven!
He came to the Ancient of Days,
And they brought Him near before Him.

14 Then to Him was given dominion and glory and a kingdom,
That all peoples, nations, and languages should serve Him.
His dominion *is* an everlasting dominion,
Which shall not pass away,
And His kingdom *the one*
Which shall not be destroyed.

Daniel's Visions Interpreted

15 "I, Daniel, was grieved in my spirit within *my* body, and the visions of my head troubled me.

16 I came near to one of those who stood by, and asked him the truth of all this. So he told me and made known to me the interpretation of these things:

17 'Those great beasts, which are four, *are* four kings *which* arise out of the earth.

18 But the saints of the Most High shall receive the kingdom, and possess the kingdom forever, even forever and ever.'

19 "Then I wished to know the truth about the fourth beast, which was different from all the others, exceedingly dreadful, *with* its teeth of iron and its nails of bronze, *which* devoured, broke in pieces, and trampled the residue with its feet;

20 and the ten horns that *were* on its head, and the other *horn* which came up, before which three fell, namely, that horn which had eyes and a mouth which spoke pompous words, whose appearance *was* greater than his fellows.

21 "I was watching; and the same horn was making war against the saints, and prevailing against them,

22 until the Ancient of Days came, and a judgment was made *in favor* of the saints of the Most High, and the time came for the saints to possess the kingdom.

23 "Thus he said:
'The fourth beast shall be
A fourth kingdom on earth,
Which shall be different from all *other* kingdoms,
And shall devour the whole earth,
Trample it and break it in pieces.

24 The ten horns *are* ten kings
Who shall arise from this kingdom.
And another shall rise after them;
He shall be different from the first *ones*,
And shall subdue three kings.

25 He shall speak *pompous* words against the Most High,
Shall persecute the saints of the Most High,
And shall intend to change times and law.
Then *the saints* shall be given into his hand

For a time and times and half a time.

26 'But the court shall be seated,
And they shall take away his dominion,
To consume and destroy *it* forever.

27 Then the kingdom and dominion,
And the greatness of the kingdoms under the whole heaven,
Shall be given to the people, the saints of the Most High.
His kingdom *is* an everlasting kingdom,
And all dominions shall serve and obey Him.'

28 "This *is* the end of the account. As for me, Daniel, my thoughts greatly troubled me, and my countenance changed; but I kept the matter in my heart."

Daniel 7:1–28	The 4 Beasts	Represents/ Meaning
Vision of the Four Beasts	1. (7:4) like a lion, and had eagle's wings. I watched till its wings were plucked off; and it was lifted up from the earth and made to stand on two feet like a man, and a man's heart was given to it	This represents the **Medo-Persian Empire**, after it had conquered by the Babylonian, which had previously conquered the Assyrian Empire. The Medo-Persian Empire contained Jews from the **Israelite nations (Israel and Judah).**
	2. (7:5) another beast, a second, like a bear. It was raised up on one side, and *had* three ribs in its mouth between its teeth. And they said thus to it: 'Arise, devour much flesh!'	The **Greek Empire** under Alexandra the Great, was fierce, having an empire that stretched from Macedonia to Egypt and from Greece to India.
	3. (7:6) there was another, like a leopard, which had on its back four wings of a bird. The beast also had four heads, and dominion was given to it.	This beast which looked like a leopard, but with four wings like a bird, having also four heads, with dominion, represents the **Roman Empire (Rome)**. The Roman Empire ruled for over 750 years, from 190 BC to 590 A.D., conquering much of the East and Western European provinces/ nations. Like Medo-Persian and Greece Empire the Roman were dominate, brutal, introducing false gods, new technologies and cultures. They controlled all land by invasion, including Israel and Jerusalem, all citizens (Jewish) with its territory. The four heads represent the **Assyrian, Babylonian, Greece and Roman Empires.**
	4. (7:7) After this I saw in the night visions, and behold, a fourth beast, dreadful and terrible, exceedingly strong. It had huge iron teeth; it was devouring, breaking in pieces, and trampling the residue with its feet. It was different from all the	Please read: Revelation 13 – The Beast from the Sea and The Beast from the Earth Revelation 14 – The Lamb and the 144,000, The Proclamations of the Three Angels, Reaping the Earth's Harvest, Reaping the Grapes of Wrath

beasts that were before it, and it had ten horns. **(7:8)** I was considering the horns, and there was another horn, a little one, coming up among them, before whom three of the first horns were plucked out by the roots. And there, in this horn, were eyes like the eyes of a man, and a mouth speaking pompous words.	The Fourth beast represents the final *One World Government/ Order*, which will be a Global Empire, where all worldwide nations the (ten horns meaning ten kingdoms/ ten continents) & governments, and their leaders will give full authority to one individual – the Antichrist. 1. **This individual will esteem himself above the entire world, having power and knowledge of resolving all Global issues affecting all nations, through his signs and wonders, never experienced before (including financial power)!** 2. **Famines, droughts, earthquakes and all worldwide climate and environmental issues will be healed because of his powers through wonders!** 3. Global populations and governments will praise and worship this man (Antichrist), and he will be seen to be as a living God. 4. Those who do not recognise him as God/ Christ will be imprisoned, tortured and murdered, their household possessions and all monies will be taken. 5. For the Antichrist will possess full control over every living person and will command that their obedience to him must be shown via a "mark" on their right hand or forehead. 6. Please note that the three horns represent England, Spain and France, part of the Roman Empire. These horns were plucked out by another horn, with eyes of a man, speaking pompous words. This one horn represents America, which was founded in 1776 by England, Spain and France, with lesser nations following afterwards.
9 "I watched till thrones were ⁴put in place, And the Ancient of Days was seated;	Daniel 7:9-10 depicts the coming of Jesus Christ, the Son of God, at the end times, predicted in **Revelation 1 and 20** **Revelation 1:9-20**

Vision of the Ancient of Days	Vision of the Son of Man
His garment *was* white as snow, And the hair of His head *was* like pure wool. His throne *was* a fiery flame, Its wheels a burning fire; **10** A fiery stream issued And came forth from before Him. A thousand thousands ministered to Him; Ten thousand times ten thousand stood before Him. The court was seated, And the books were opened.	⁹I, John, both your brother and companion in the tribulation and kingdom and patience of Jesus Christ, was on the island that is called Patmos for the word of God and for the testimony of Jesus Christ. ¹⁰I was in the Spirit on the Lord's Day, and I heard behind me a loud voice, as of a trumpet, ¹¹ saying, "I am the Alpha and the Omega, the First and the Last," and, "What you see, write in a book and send *it* to the seven churches which are in Asia: to Ephesus, to Smyrna, to Pergamos, to Thyatira, to Sardis, to Philadelphia, and to Laodicea." ¹²Then I turned to see the voice that spoke with me. And having turned I saw seven golden lampstands, ¹³ and in the midst of the seven lampstands *One* like the Son of Man, clothed with a garment down to the feet and girded about the chest with a golden band. ¹⁴His head and hair were white like wool, as white as snow, and His eyes like a flame of fire; ¹⁵His feet were like fine brass, as if refined in a furnace, and His voice as the sound of many waters; ¹⁶He had in His right hand seven stars, out of His mouth went a sharp two-edged sword, and His countenance *was* like the sun shining in its strength. ¹⁷And when I saw Him, I fell at His feet as dead. But He laid His right hand on me, saying to me, "Do not be afraid; I am the First and the Last. ¹⁸I *am* He who lives, and was dead, and behold, I am alive forevermore. Amen. And I have the keys of Hades and of Death. ¹⁹Write the things which you have seen, and the things which are, and the things which will take place after this. ²⁰ The mystery of the seven stars which you saw in My right hand, and the seven golden lampstands: The seven stars are the angels of the seven churches, and the seven lampstands which you saw are the seven churches.

Revelation 20:11-15

The Great White Throne Judgment
¹¹Then I saw a great white throne and Him who sat on it, from whose face the earth and the heaven fled away. And there was found no place for them. ¹²And I saw the dead, small and great, standing before God, and books were opened. And another book |

	was opened, which is *the Book of Life*. And the dead were judged according to their works, by the things which were written in the books. **13** The sea gave up the dead who were in it, and Death and Hades delivered up the dead who were in them. And they were judged, each one according to his works. **14** Then Death and Hades were cast into the lake of fire. This is the second death. **15** And anyone not found written in the Book of Life was cast into the lake of fire. **Please read:** Revelation 13 – The Beast from the Sea and The Beast from the Earth Revelation 14 – The Lamb and the 144,000, The Proclamations of the Three Angels, Reaping the Earth's Harvest, Reaping the Grapes of Wrath Revelation 17 – The Scarlet Woman and the Scarlet Beast Verses 7-11 "(7) But the angel said to me, "Why did you marvel? I will tell you the [a]mystery of the woman and of the beast that carries her, which has the seven heads and the ten horns". ***The seven heads are Empires at that specific biblical times: Egypt, Assyria, Babylon, Medo-Persia, Greece, Rome and the final New World Order (beast and Antichrist). The ten horns represents the ten continents of the world, when the world has grown from the past empires, with final global empire!*** (8) The beast represents Satan as a man on earth (beast that you saw was, and is not, and will ascend out of the bottomless pit, and go to perdition). And those who dwell on the earth will marvel, whose names are not written in the Book of Life from the foundation of the world, when they see the beast that was, and is not, and yet is.
11 "I watched then because of the sound of the pompous words which the horn was speaking; I watched till the beast was slain, and its body destroyed and given to the burning flame. **12** As for the rest of the beasts, they had their dominion taken away, yet their lives were prolonged for a season and a time.	

(9) Here *is* the mind which has wisdom: The seven heads are seven mountains on which the woman sits. *(**The seven heads are Empires at those specific biblical times: Egypt, Assyria, Babylon, Medo-Persia, Greece, Rome and the final One World Order (beast and Antichrist)**.*

(10) There are also seven kings. Five have fallen, one is, *and* the other has not yet come. And when he comes, he must continue a short time. ¹¹ The beast that was, and is not, is himself also the eighth, and is of the seven, and is going to ⁽ᵃ⁾perdition.

(Israel and Judah were carried away to: Assyria, then Babylon, Medo-Persia, Greece and finally Roman Empires. These <u>five kings</u> (kingdoms/ empires) fell and are no longer.

The sixth empire will be the Global New World Order. The beast that was and is not represents Satan as a man on earth (Antichrist). The Antichrist will be thrown into the lake of fire/ perdition.

Christ Jesus returns to earth with His Angels, to conquer the sixth empire, having been given dominion over the entire world for 1,000 years, and Satan will be chained in hell until he is released after this time.

After he is released, Satan will stir a final battle with those in the world who oppose Christ. Christ will conquer Satan, and Satan will be thrown into the lake of fire, with all those who are against Christ. Therefore, Satan is the eighth himself, and is of the seven!! *(Revelation 20)*.

13 "I was watching in the night visions,
And behold, *One like the Son of Man,*
Coming with the clouds of heaven!

		Please read Revelation 19:1-19			
	He came to the Ancient of Days, And they brought Him near before Him.				
	14 Then to Him was given dominion and glory and a kingdom, That all peoples, nations, and languages should serve Him. His dominion *is* an everlasting dominion, Which shall not pass away, And His kingdom *the one* Which shall not be destroyed.	Please read Revelation 19, 21 (All Things Made New) and 22 (River of Life)			
Daniel's Visions Interpreted	**15** "I, Daniel, was grieved in my spirit within *my* body, and the visions of my head troubled me. **16** I came near to one of those who stood by, and asked him the truth of all this. So he told me and made known to me the interpretation of these things: **17** 'Those great beasts, which are four, *are* four kings *which* arise out of the earth.		Statue	Represent	The Great Beasts/ Four Kings (Meaning/ Empire
			1	Gold,	Head	Assyrian Empire
			2	Silver	Arms	Babylonian Empire
			3	Bronze	Belly and Thighs	Medo-Persian Empire, Greek Empire
			4	Iron and Clay	Legs and Feet	1. Roman Empire 2. One World Government/ Order (Global Empire)

~ 142 ~

18 But the saints of the Most High shall receive the kingdom, and possess the kingdom forever, even forever and ever.'	Please read Revelation 19 (Heaven Exults over Babylon), 20 (Satan Bound 1,000), 21 (All Things Made New) and 22 (River of Life)
19 "Then I wished to know the truth about the fourth beast, which was different from all the others, exceedingly dreadful, *with its* teeth of iron and its nails of bronze, *which* devoured, broke in pieces, and trampled the residue with its feet;	Please read Revelation 11 & 12 with 13 **Revelation 13** **(The Beast from the Sea)** (1) Then I stood on the sand of the sea. And I saw a beast rising up out of the sea, having seven heads and ten horns, and on his horns ten crowns, and on his heads a blasphemous name. *(Note: The ten horns meaning ten kingdoms/ ten continents of worldwide governments, and their leaders).*
20 and the ten horns that *were* on its head, and the other *horn* which came up, before which three fell, namely, that horn which had eyes and a mouth which spoke ²pompous words, whose appearance *was* greater than his fellows.	(2) Now the beast which I saw was like a leopard, his feet were like *the feet of* a bear, and his mouth like the mouth of a lion. The dragon gave him his power, his throne, and great authority. (3) And I saw one of his heads as if it had been mortally wounded, and his deadly wound was healed. And all the world marvelled and followed the beast. (4) So they worshiped the dragon who gave authority to the beast; and they worshiped the beast, saying, "Who *is* like the beast? Who is able to make war with him?"
21 "I was watching; and the same horn was making war against the saints, and prevailing against them,	(5) And he was given a mouth speaking great things and blasphemies, and he was given authority to continue for forty-two months. *(3.1/2 Years)*
22 until the Ancient of Days came, and a judgment was made *in*	*(Note: Please note that the three horns represent England, Spain and France, part of Roman Empire. These horns were plucked out by another horn, with eyes of a man, speaking pompous words. This one horn represents America, which was founded in 1776 by England, Spain and France, with lesser nations following afterwards).*

favour of the saints of the Most High, and the time came for the saints to possess the kingdom. **(Note: Please read Revelation 19:1-19)** 23 "Thus he said: 'The fourth beast shall be A fourth kingdom on earth, Which shall be different from all *other* kingdoms, And shall devour the whole earth, Trample it and break it in pieces. 24 The ten horns *are* ten kings Who shall arise from this kingdom. And another shall rise after them;	(6) Then he opened his mouth in blasphemy against God, to blaspheme His name, His tabernacle, and those who dwell in heaven. (7) It was granted to him to make war with the saints and to overcome them. And authority was given to him over every tribe, tongue, and nation. *(Note: All Christians, who believe and followers in Christ Jesus, called "saints" will be persecuted by the beast and the world).* (8) All who dwell on the earth will worship him, whose names have not been written in the Book of Life of the Lamb slain from the foundation of the world. (9) If anyone has an ear, let him hear. (10) He who leads into captivity shall go into captivity; he who kills with the sword must be killed with the sword. Here is the patience and the faith of the saints. **The Beast from the Earth** (11) Then I saw another beast coming up out of the earth, and he had two horns like a lamb and spoke like a dragon. *(Note: Antichrist)* (12) And he exercises all the authority of the first beast in his presence, and causes the earth and those who dwell in it to worship the first beast, whose deadly wound was healed. *(Note: The ten horns meaning ten kingdoms - The fourth "beast" kingdom meaning One World/ Global Empire, being different from the first Empires, subduing those three kings and Empires (i.e. England, France, Spain, and all nations under the Assyrian, Babylonian, Medo-Persian, Greek and Roman Empires).* (13) He performs great signs, so that he even makes fire come down from heaven on the earth in the sight of men. *(Note:* *1. This individual will esteem himself above the entire world, having power and knowledge of resolving all Global issues affecting all nations, through*

He shall be different from the first *ones*, And shall subdue three kings. 25 He shall speak *pompous* words against the Most High, Shall persecute the saints of the Most High, And shall intend to change times and law. Then *the saints* shall be given into his hand For a time and times and half a time. 26 'But the court shall be seated, And they shall take away his dominion, To consume and destroy *it* forever.	his signs and wonders, never experienced before (including financial global powers)! 2. Famines, droughts, earthquakes and all worldwide climate and environmental issues will be healed because of his powers through wonders! 3. **Global populations and governments will praise and worship this man (Antichrist), and he will be seen to be as a living God.** (14) And he deceives those who dwell on the earth by those signs which he was granted to do in the sight of the beast, telling those who dwell on the earth to make an image to the beast who was wounded by the sword and lived. (15) He was granted *power* to give breath to the image of the beast, that the image of the beast should both speak and cause as many as would not worship the image of the beast to be killed. *(Note: Those who do not recognise him as God/ Christ will be imprisoned, tortured and murdered, their household possessions and all monies will be taken.)* (16) He causes all, both small and great, rich and poor, free and slave, to receive a mark on their right hand or on their foreheads, (17) and that no one may buy or sell except one who has the mark or the name of the beast, or the number of his name.

(Note: *For the Antichrist will possess full control over every nation and person, commanding their obedience to him must be shown via a "mark" on their right hand or forehead.)*

(18) Here is wisdom. Let him who has understanding calculate the number of the beast, for it is the number of a man: His number *is* 666.

(Note: *The number 666 is a term meaning "man of authority" to a one ruler.*

During the time of the Roman Empire, Christians who did not conform to the Roman practices of believing on their many gods, were persecuted and murdered for their faith they had in Christ Jesus. Because of their deaths, Christians were seen as martyrs or saints.

It is known that Jesus, the Son of God was crucified on the cross, because the Jewish Church and Chiefs (Pharisees and Sadducees), did not believe that Jesus was the Christ, the Son of God (even though Christ was prophesised in the Old Testament).

Therefore, when Christ was captured at the garden of Gethsemane, he was taken to the Chief Priests, to be questioned about who he was (even though he was known of all the great miracles, prophesising to the Jews daily, the many wonders he done, visiting the temple in Jerusalem).

Because of their (Jews) lack of faith, Jesus was sent to Pilate, the Roman Governor, who questioned him regarding the Chief Priests statements that Jesus was the King of the Jews and opposed Caesar as King. Therefore, Jesus was crucified at Golgotha or Calvary, fulfilling God's prophecy that the Son of God must die on the cross, so that those who believe will inherit eternal life! Therefore, Jesus died during the Roman Empire Tiberius reign.

The Antichrist will rise up out Rome, will be an non-practicing Jewish man (Roman Catholic POPE.....?). He will have great wisdom, power and charisma, demonstrating the many signs and wonders over the entire world, those of leaders and inter-faith groups. All authority will be given to him for seven years, and that all nations and peoples will bow, wanting to their allegiance (mark of the beast) for he will be seen as god, wanting to preside in the rebuilt temple in Jerusalem, after the 3.1/2 years.

However, he will break his promise of peace halfway through the seven years, and all nations will oppose Jerusalem.

The two witnesses (Revelation 11) who are Enoch and Elijah will stand in the holy city for forty-two months, but the Antichrist will kill them both, as they oppose him from gaining entry into the holy temple. Such the temple will be rebuilt!

It is at this time, the tribulation will commence, the returning of our Lord Jesus Christ, and all His heaven Kingdom to battle with the Antichrist.

The beast that was and is not represents Satan as a man on earth (Antichrist). The Antichrist will be thrown into the lake of fire/ perdition.

Christ Jesus returns to earth with His Angels, to conquer the sixth empire, having been given dominion over the entire world for 1,000 years, and Satan will be chained in hell until he is released after this time.

27 Then the kingdom and dominion,

	After he is released, Satan will stir a final battle with those in the world who oppose Christ. Christ will conquer Satan, and Satan will be thrown into the lake of fire, with all those who are against Christ. Therefore, Satan is the eighth himself, and is of the seven!! *(Revelation 20)*. **Please read Revelation 14 to 22**
And the greatness of the kingdoms under the whole heaven, Shall be given to the people, the saints of the Most High. His kingdom *is* an everlasting kingdom, And all dominions shall serve and obey Him.' **28** "This *is* the end of the account. As for me, Daniel, my thoughts greatly troubled me, and my countenance changed; but I kept the matter in my heart."	

2 John 1: 7-11 For many deceivers have gone out into the world who do not confess Jesus Christ as coming in the flesh. This is a deceiver and an antichrist. **8** Look to yourselves, that we do not lose those things we worked for, but that we may receive a full reward. **9** Whoever transgresses and does not abide in the doctrine of Christ does not have God. He who abides in the doctrine of Christ has both the Father and the Son. **10** If anyone comes to you and does not bring this doctrine, do not receive him into your house nor greet him; **11** for he who greets him shares in his evil deeds.

None Will Escape

No person can escape the judgment! All who have ever lived will be there. All who are now living will be there. All who will live in the future will be there. The rich will be judged, the poor will be judged. Kings, presidents, and the common man will be judged. All will be judged alike. **"We must all appear before the judgment seat of Christ, that each one may receive . . . according to what he has done, whether good or bad"** (*2 Corinthians 5:10*).

According To Our Works

We will be judged according to our works! All the good things we have done will be revealed. All of the bad things we have done will be revealed. **"Who will render to each one according to his deeds: eternal life to those who by patient continuance in doing good seek for glory, honour; and immortality; but to those who . . . do not obey . . . indignation and wrath"** (***Romans 2:6-8***).

e. Hell

All the wicked and all who have never obeyed the gospel of Jesus Christ will be cast into Hell.

Hell is a place which was prepared for the Devil and his angels. "**Then He will also say to those on the left hand, Depart from Me, you cursed, into everlasting fire prepared for the devil and his angels**" (*Matthew 25:41*).

Hell is a terrible place! The Bible uses three pictures to tell us how terrible Hell is:

- First, Hell is often described as a **fire** which never stops burning. Jesus said, "**And if your eye causes you to sin, pluck it out. It is better for you to enter the kingdom of God with one eye, rather than having two eyes, to be cast into hell fire - where the worm does not die, and the fire is not quenched**" (*Mark 9:47-48*).

- Second, Hell is often described as a place of great **darkness** where people in pain and anguish weep and gnash their teeth, "**And cast the unprofitable servant into outer darkness. There will be weeping and gnashing of teeth**" (*Matthew 25:30*).

- Third, Hell is described as **the second death**. "**But the cowardly, unbelieving, abominable, murderers, sexually immoral, sorcerers, idolaters, and all liars shall have their part in the lake which burns with fire and brimstone, which is the second death**" (*Revelation 21:8*).

Hell is eternal! Those cast into Hell will be punished forever and ever. Jesus said, "**And these will go away into everlasting punishment, but the righteous into eternal life**" (*Matthew 25:46*).

The Bible plainly teaches that Hell is a real place. It is a place of punishment for the wicked and for all who do not obey Christ. "**You who are troubled rest with us when the Lord Jesus is revealed from heaven with His mighty angels, in flaming fire taking vengeance on those who do not know God, and . . . do not obey the gospel** of our Lord Jesus Christ. These shall be punished with everlasting destruction from the presence of the Lord and from the glory of His power" (*2 Thessalonians 1:7-9*).

f. Heaven

On the Day of Judgment, the wicked and unbelievers will be cast into Hell, but the faithful Christians will receive eternal life. They will be given a home in Heaven which Jesus has prepared for them. "**In My Father's house are many mansions . . . I go to prepare a place for you . . . I will come again and receive you to Myself; that where I am, there you may be also. And where I go you know, and the way you know**" (*John 14:2-4*).

Jesus is now preparing a place in Heaven for us if we will become his faithful disciples. Heaven is a beautiful place. In Heaven there are no bad things. There is no pain, sickness, sadness, trouble, or death. There is no hate or fear in Heaven. In Heaven there is only peace and happiness and every good thing.

The apostle John tells us about this beautiful home which Jesus is preparing for us. "**I, John, saw the holy city . . . coming down out of heaven from God, prepared as a bride adorned for her husband . . . I heard a loud voice from heaven saying, Behold, the tabernacle of God is with men . . . God Himself will be with them and be their God. And God will wipe away every tear from their eyes; there shall be no more death, nor sorrow, nor crying. There shall be no more pain, for the former things have passed away**" (*Revelation 21:1-4*). Read Revelation 21 and Revelation 22, for a full description of the beautiful place called Heaven.

What about you? Are you prepared for the judgment? Prepare now so that you can have a home with Jesus in Heaven, becoming a Christian, a member of Christ's church, **"which He purchased with His own blood"** (*Acts 20:28*).

CHAPTER 7

References

The following references are from the (NKJV) New Kings James Version Bible, and publications.

Please note that biblical references to the Bible, will be quoted back to that Book, and relevant Chapter and Verse i.e. Genesis 1:1 (chapter 1, verse 1).

Where only a book and chapter has been referenced, then this will be shown as Genesis 1.

1. John 3:16
2. Malachi 3:6
3. John 3:16-18
4. Revelation 21:1-8
5. 2 Thessalonians 2:7-12

Chapter 1 – Introduction

6. Psalms 8:4
7. Job 14:1-2
8. 1 Thessalonians 5:23
9. Genesis 3:19
10. Genesis 35:18
11. James 2:26
12. Ecclesiastes 12:7

13. 1 John 2:15-17
14. Matthew 16:26
15. Ecclesiastes 12:13
16. Hebrews 9:27
17. Romans 14:12
18. 2 Corinthians 5:10
19. John 14:1-3
20. 2 Corinthians 4:16 & 5:6
21. Philippians 3:20
22. Revelation 21:3-5
23. Matthew 10:28
24. Matthew 25:41,46
25. 2 Thessalonians 1:7-10
26. John 3:16
27. Matthew 11:28-29
28. John 8:24
29. Luke 13:3
30. Romans 10:9-10
31. Acts 8:37
32. Romans 6:3-5
33. Acts 2:38
34. 2 Corinthians 5:17

Chapter 2 - GOD
a. God

35. Genesis 1:1
36. Psalm 90:2
37. Hebrews 1:10-12
38. Genesis 18:14
39. Proverbs 5:21
40. 1 John 3:20

41. Luke 24:39
42. 1 John 1:5
43. 1 John 4:8
44. 1 John 4:10
45. Leviticus 19:2
46. Psalm 11:7
47. Psalm 103:8
48. Psalm 19:1
49. Romans 2:14-16
50. Hebrews 1:1-2
51. 2 Timothy 3:16-17
52. 2 Peter 1:21
53. John 17:17
54. John 16:13
55. Jeremiah 10:23
56. Hebrews 9:27
57. John 12:48
58. Matthew 16:27
59. 2 Corinthians 5:10
60. Romans 1:16
61. Hebrews 5:9
62. Mark 16:16
63. Acts 2:38
64. Galatians 1:8
65. 2 John 9

Chapter 3 - The Downfall of Lucifer/ The Angel of Light

66. Revelation 12:7-9
67. Ezekiel 28:12-18
68. Isaiah 14:12-20
69. Matthew 24:24

70. John 8:43-45
71. John 8:47
72. John 17:14
73. Ephesians 2:1-3
74. Ephesians 6:11-12
75. 2 Corinthians 11:3-4
76. 2 Corinthians 11:14
77. 1 John 5:18-19
78. 2 Thessalonians 2:3
79. 2 Thessalonians 2:6-7
80. 2 Thessalonians 2:10
81. James 3:15-16
82. 1 Peter 5:6
83. 1 Peter 5:8-9
84. Revelation 12:4
85. Revelation 12:12

Chapter 4 - The Old Testament

a. The Old Testament
86. Romans 15:4
87. I Corinthians 10:11
88. 2 Peter 1:21

b. The books of the Law, History, Poetry and Prophecy
89. Genesis, Exodus, Leviticus, Numbers, and Deuteronomy (Old Testament, The Books of the Law)
90. Exodus 19:3
91. Deuteronomy 5:1
92. Matthew 5:17-18
93. Galatians 3:23-28
94. Colossians 2:13-14

95. Joshua, Judges, Ruth, 1 and 2 Samuel, 1 and 2 Kings, 1 and 2 Chronicles, Ezra, Nehemiah, and Esther (Old Testament, The Books of History)
96. Job, Psalms, Proverbs, Ecclesiastes, and Song of Solomon (Old Testament, The Books of Poetry)
97. Isaiah, Jeremiah, Lamentations, Ezekiel, Daniel, Hosea, Joel, Amos, Obadiah, Jonah, Micah, Nahum, Habakkuk, Zephaniah, Haggai, Zechariah, and Malachi (Old Testament, The Books of Prophecy)

c. The Fall of Mankind and Why?

98. Genesis 1-4
99. Genesis 3:14-19
100. Romans 16:20

d. Sin, what changed?

101. 1 John 3:4
102. 1 John 5:17
103. Romans 3:23
104. Hebrews 3:13
105. James 1:14- 15
106. Galatians 5:19-21
107. Hebrews 10:25
108. 2 Thessalonians 1:8
109. John 14:6
110. Mark 16:16

e. God's Commandments, Judgements and Laws

111. Genesis 1:26-31
112. Genesis 2:7
113. Psalm 139:14
114. Psalm 82:6

115. John 10:34-36
116. Genesis Chapters, 2-3
117. Genesis 3:15
118. Malachi 3:1-6

f. The Ten Commandments
119. Exodus 20:1-17

g. Bible verses about Judgement
120. Romans 2:1
121. Matthew 7:1
122. Proverbs 21:2
123. Romans 14:13
124. Matthew 12:36
125. Matthew 7:3
126. Luke 6:37
127. Romans 14:4
128. Isaiah 54:17
129. James 4:12
130. Romans 2:12
131. Hebrews 13:4
132. John 3:17
133. Colossians 2:16-17
134. Revelation 20:12-13
135. Romans 14:3
136. Romans 8:1-2
137. 1 Corinthians 9:27
138. John 3:18
139. Isaiah 26:9
140. Romans 6:23
141. James 5:12
142. Mark 16:16
143. 2 Peter 2:9

144. 2 Timothy 4:7-8

h. Abomination to God laws
145. Leviticus 18:22
146. Leviticus 20:13
147. Romans 1:18-32
148. Deuteronomy 22:5
149. Proverbs 6:16-19
150. Luke 16:15
151. Leviticus 7:18
152. Daniel 11:31
153. Revelation 21:27
154. Deuteronomy 17:1
155. 1 Kings 11:5
156. Daniel 12:11
157. Proverbs 12:22
158. Genesis 43:32
159. Deuteronomy 7:25
160. Proverbs 11:1
161. Daniel 9:27
162. Leviticus 19:27
163. Genesis 46:34
164. Proverbs 13:19
165. Isaiah 1:13
166. Leviticus 7:21
167. Deuteronomy 23:18
168. 1 Kings 14:24
169. Matthew 24:15
170. Mark 13:14
171. Proverbs 29:27
172. Leviticus 11:20
173. Leviticus 11:23

174. Leviticus 11:41
175. Leviticus 11:42
176. Isaiah 66:17
177. Deuteronomy 27:15
178. 2 Kings 23:13
179. Proverbs 15:8
180. Isaiah 44:19
181. Jeremiah 32:35
182. Ezekiel 22:11
183. Proverbs 3:32
184. Proverbs 11:20
185. Deuteronomy 22:23-24
186. Exodus 10:2
187. Deuteronomy 12:31
188. Leviticus 11:13
189. Exodus 8:26
190. Exodus 21:7
191. Proverbs 16:5
192. Mark 7:20-23
193. Deuteronomy 24:1-4
194. Jeremiah 6:15
195. Deuteronomy 25:13-16
196. Proverbs 20:10
197. Leviticus 11:12
198. Leviticus 20:14
199. Revelation 21:8
200. Deuteronomy 7:25-26
201. Leviticus 18:29
202. Exodus 8:22
203. Deuteronomy 25:16
204. Proverbs 6:16
205. Proverbs 24:9

206. Proverbs 17:15
207. Leviticus 11:10-13
208. Leviticus 11:10-12
209. Leviticus 11:11
210. Deuteronomy 7:26
211. Exodus 35:2
212. Leviticus 11:10
213. Proverbs 28:9
214. 1 Corinthians 6:9
215. Galatians 3:23-25
216. Exodus 20:13
217. Deuteronomy 18:12
218. Jeremiah 32:34
219. Proverbs 8:13
220. Proverbs 6:17
221. Ezekiel 8:6

Chapter 5 - The New Testament

a. The New Testament

222. Matthew, Mark, Luke, and John (The Gospels)
223. Acts (The Apostles)
224. Acts 2:36-38, 41, 42, 47 People on day of Pentecost
225. Acts 8:1-13 People of Samaria
226. Acts 8:26-39 Ethiopian Eunuch
227. Acts 9:1-19; Acts 22:1-16 Saul of Tarsus, who became the apostle Paul
228. Acts 10:1-48 Cornelius
229. Acts 16:25-34 Philippian jailer
230. Romans, 1 and 2 Corinthians, Galatians, Ephesians, Philippians, Colossians, 1 and 2 Thessalonians, 1 and 2 Timothy, Titus, and Philemon (The Epistles)

231. Romans: Chapters 1-11
232. Romans: Chapters 12-16
233. 1 and 2 Corinthians
234. Galatians
235. Ephesians
236. 1 and 2 Thessalonians
237. 1 and 2 Timothy and Titus
238. Philemon
239. Hebrews
240. James; 1 and 2 Peter, 1, 2, and 3 John; Jude

b. The Two Covenants
241. Exodus 20:1-17
242. Exodus 21-23
243. Exodus 24:7
244. Exodus 24:8
245. Hebrews 8:6-7
246. Romans 7:7
247. Galatians 3:24
248. Hebrews 10:9
249. Colossians 2:14
250. Matthew 5:17
251. Luke 24:44
252. Acts 13:29
253. Hebrews 9:15
254. Galatians 3:28

c. Jesus Christ, The Son of God, The Saviour
255. Genesis 3:15
256. Luke 1:31,34-35
257. Luke 2:52
258. Hebrews 4:15
259. Mark 1:15

260. Mark 1:34-35
261. Mark 10:46-52
262. Mark 6:34-44
263. Luke 7:11-16
264. John 11
265. Acts 2:22
266. Matthew 13
267. Luke 15
268. Matthew 16
269. Matthew 16:18
270. Daniel 2:44
271. Acts 20:28
272. Ephesians 5:23
273. Ephesians 1:22
274. Matthew 16:21
275. 1 Corinthians 15:3-4

d. Faith
276. Hebrews 11:6
277. Hebrews 11:1
278. Romans 10:17
279. Romans 10:14
280. Matthew 8:26
281. Matthew 15:28
282. Acts 16:30-31
283. James 2:19
284. Mark 16:16
285. James 2:24

e. Repentance
286. Acts 17:30-31
287. Matthew 21:28-29
288. 2 Corinthians 7:10
289. Romans 2:4
290. Luke 3:8
291. 2 Peter 3:9
292. Acts 2:38

f. Confession
293. Romans 10:9-10
294. Acts 8:35-37
295. Matthew 10:32-33
296. Acts 5:29
297. 1 Peter 2:21
298. James 5:16
299. 1 John 1:9

g. Baptism
300. Mark 16:16
301. Romans 10:17
302. Acts 2:38
303. Romans 10:9-10
304. Acts 8:12
305. Romans 6:4
306. John 3:23
307. Acts 8:38-39
308. Mark 16:16
309. 1 Peter 3:21
310. Acts 2:38
311. Galatians 3:27
312. Ephesians 1:22-23
313. 1 Corinthians 12:13

314. Acts 20:7
315. Acts 2:42
316. 2 Tim. 4:1-5

h. The Church, Part 1
317. Matthew 16:18-19
318. Acts 2:1-47
319. Luke 24:46-47
320. Ephesians 2:19-21
321. 1 Kings 8:12-13
322. 1 Corinthians 3:16-17
323. 1 Timothy 3:15
324. John 3:5
325. 1 Peter 2:9
326. Ephesians 1:22-23
327. Ephesians 4:4

i. The Church, Part 2
328. 1 Corinthians 1:1-2
329. Acts 20:28
330. Romans 16:16
331. Acts 5:14
332. 1 Timothy 4:12
333. 1 Corinthians 1:2
334. Philippians 1:1
335. Acts 11:26
336. Acts 20:7
337. Acts 11:26
338. Acts 26:28
339. 1 Peter 4:14-16
340. Ephesians 1:22-23
341. 2 Timothy 3:16-17
342. 1 Timothy 3:1

343. Ephesians 4:11-12
344. Acts 14:23
345. Philippians 1:1
346. 1 Timothy 3:1-7
347. Titus 1:5-10
348. 1 Timothy 3:8-13
349. Acts 20:7
350. 1 Corinthians 16:2
351. Revelation 1:10
352. Acts 20:7
353. Matthew 26:26-29
354. 1 Corinthians 11:23-26
355. Ephesians 5:19
356. Colossians 3:16
357. 1 Timothy 2:1-2
358. 1 Timothy 4:13
359. 1 Corinthians 16:2

j. The Genealogy from Adam to Jesus Christ
360. Deut. 25:5-6
361. Matthew 1:1-17
362. Luke 3:23:38

Chapter 6 - FINAL The End Times/ Prophecy
a. The Second Coming of Christ
363. Revelation 1:3
364. Genesis 3
365. Revelation 2:7
366. Revelation 1:1
367. Revelation 2:1; 2:8; 2:12; 2:18; 3:1; 3:7; 3:14; 14:13; 19:9
368. Matthew 10:1-4
369. Revelation 1:9-11

370. Revelation 11:1
371. Galatians 5:19-21
372. Revelation 2:4
373. Revelation 3:1-2
374. Revelation 3:14-16
375. Revelation 1:4
376. Revelation 2 & 3
377. Acts 19 & 20
378. Romans 8:37
379. John 14:2:3
380. Matthew 24:36
381. 1 Thessalonians 5:2
382. Acts 1:11
383. Revelation 1:7
384. 1 Thessalonians 4:16
385. John 5:28-29
386. 1 Thessalonians 4:16-17
387. 1 Corinthians 15:24
388. 2 Peter 3:10
389. Acts 17:30-31

b. Daniel and King Nebuchadnezzar Dream
390. Daniel 1:17
391. Daniel 1:19-21
392. Daniel 2:31-33
393. Daniel 2:34-35
394. 1 Kings 11:1-43
395. 2 Kings 17:5-23
396. Jeremiah 39:1-18

c. The Medo-Persian Empire
397. 2 Chronicles 36:23
398. Daniel 8:21-24

399. Daniel 7:4-7
400. Daniel 7:13-14

d. Daniel and Revelation –The Four Beasts
401. Daniel 7:1–28
402. Daniel Chapter 7:4-8
    Vision of the Four Beasts
403. Revelation 13
    The Beast from the Sea and The Beast from the Earth
404. Revelation 14 –
    The Lamb and the 144,000, The Proclamations of the Three Angels, Reaping the Earth's Harvest, Reaping the Grapes of Wrath
405. America founded, 1776
406. Daniel Chapter 7:9-14
    Vision of the Ancient of Days
407. Daniel 7:9-10
    Depicts the coming of Jesus Christ, the Son of God, at the end times, predicted in Revelation 1 and 20
408. Revelation 1:9-20
    Vision of the Son of Man
409. Revelation 20:11-15
    The Great White Throne Judgement
410. Daniel 7:11
411. Revelation 13
    The Beast from the Sea and The Beast from the Earth
412. Revelation 14
    The Lamb and the 144,000, The Proclamations of the Three Angels, Reaping the Earth's Harvest, Reaping the Grapes of Wrath
413. Daniel 7:12
414. Revelation 17:7-11

The Scarlet Woman and the Scarlet Beast
415. Revelation 20
416. Daniel 7:13-14
417. Revelation 19
     Heaven Exults over Babylon
418. Revelation 21
     All Things Made New
419. Revelation 22
     River of Life
420. Daniel 7:15-28
     Daniel's Visions Interpreted
421. Daniel 7:15-18
422. Revelation 19
     Heaven Exults over Babylon
423. Revelation 20
     Satan Bound 1,000 Years
424. Revelation 21
     All Things Made New
425. Revelation 22
     River of Life
426. Daniel 7:19-26
427. Revelation 11
428. Revelation 12
429. Revelation 13:1-18
430. Revelation 19:1-19
431. Daniel 7:27-28
432. Revelation 20
433. Revelation 14 to 22
434. 2 John 1: 7-11
435. 2 Corinthians 5:10
436. Romans 2:6-8

e. Hell
437. Matthew 25:41
438. Mark 9:47-48
439. Matthew 25:30
440. Revelation 21:8
441. Matthew 25:46
442. 2 Thessalonians 1:7-9

f. Heaven
443. John 14:2-4
444. Revelation 21:1-4
445. Acts 20:28

www.ingramcontent.com/pod-product-compliance
Lightning Source LLC
LaVergne TN
LVHW020133080526
838202LV00047B/3929